The Taming of Technology

of

by David Loth

and Morris L. Ernst

New York Simon and Schuster

First printing

SBN 671-21199-4
Library of Congress Catalog Card Number: 72-76986
Designed by Edith Fowler
Manufactured in the United States of America

Contents

| Authors' Note

The changing nature of both law and technology produces ever new confrontations between them. Some of those narrated in the following pages had not been finally resolved as this was written—and others may never be. The record is up to date as of this time, however.

D.L.
M.L.E.

February 1, 1972

INTRODUCTION

1 | Law's Mysterious Ways

As long as Science seemed a universal benefactor, Law accommodated to new machines and processes with a minimum of control over them. But as technology spun off material blessings at an ever accelerating pace, unexpectedly unpleasant side effects gave Science some of the sinister aspects that Law had to curb in absolute governments and later in unrestrained corporate enterprise. In those earlier days, bureaucrats and company executives cried out that Law was ruining them. Law converted both governments and corporations to more faithful service of society than either could have achieved unrestrained. She can do the same for Science and in certain ways has already begun to do so.

The probable means are regulations to delay the hasty application of scientific discoveries until the scientists are reasonably sure of the effects. Then Law can forbid the most harmful ones. In time she may force technology to find ways to produce energy cleanly, to fuel a motor car with something that does not poison the air, to make paper without fouling rivers, to recycle bottles, cans and other wastes before we are smothered by them.

Legal paths toward such reforms vary, for Law is unpredictable and infinitely variable. Generally she checks reckless plunges into the future by the strong hand of the past, countering tomorrow's technology with yesterday's instruments.

Law and Science stage their more dramatic confrontations when a new product or technique, hailed as a servant of mankind, goes on a rampage of unforeseen side effects. Detergents, one remembers, were said to have done more for women's liberation than the vote. We still hear that the weekly wash becomes whiter and brighter and cleaner with no need for human labor. But after one of the ingredients, phosphate, has done its work in the washing machine, it goes into the ground water or the nearest lake or river where, if not expensively treated first, it kills the water.

Science seldom corrects such conditions until people call on Law. When an earlier detergent problem became acute in 1964, Science waited until Congress was considering, and several states and localities had already passed, bills to outlaw detergents that foamed. A major ingredient then was a chemical called alkyl benzene sulfonate, and it produced suds of spectacular dimensions. One day the Rock River in Illinois carried so much of the stuff over a handsome waterfall that a wall of foam forty feet high formed at the bottom and drifted majestically downstream. In many parts of the country, water from household taps sported a head as frothy as that of the best beer. Industry, which that year sold a billion pounds of detergents for more than a billion dollars, spent $150,000,000 to find a substitute for alkyl benzene sulfonate and to change equipment, beating the 1965 deadline in the new laws. Five years later, the phosphate crisis led Suffolk County in New York, Chicago, and a number of smaller places to forbid sale of detergents that contain this substance.

Law's authority to tell manufacturers what they can sell to householders for use in their own sinks was established only after courts rose to the challenge of technology. By now, what is called the police power is so well settled that the detergent industry did not bother to protest that such local ordinances violated their sacred rights. That issue had been settled three-quarters of a century earlier when the establishment rather than the people resisted technology. One of the decisive battles was a lawsuit entitled *Health Department v. the Rector and Trustees of Trinity Church*, decided by the Supreme Court in 1895. The church, a New York landmark for three-hundred years, was and is the owner of extensive urban real estate acquired at a time when Wall Street marked the northern boundary of the metropolis. In the 1890's, much of this land was covered by five-story tenements. Each had its own water supply—a tap or a well—in its backyard and a privy for the tenants.

A reform administration, elected in one of the rare defeats of Tammany Hall when New York City consisted mainly of Manhattan Island, was scientifically minded. It adopted an ordinance requiring all tenements to have running water indoors, with at least one tap on every floor that was "occupied or intended to be occupied." Landlords denounced this as a moral outrage and an unconstitutional invasion of a property owner's rights. The trustees of Trinity Church decided to fight it through the courts to the bitter end, in this instance, the Supreme Court.

Impressive precedent supported the church's position. Its lawyers argued that although the city might be empowered to impose the frippery of running water on every floor in new buildings, the expense in existing structures violated the much pleaded Fifth Amendment's concluding clause: "nor shall private property be taken for public use, without just compensation." Even if the court held that the legislature could legally confiscate in this way, surely it could not delegate the power to the Health Department, which had been designated as the enforcement agency. At the very least, the argument ran, the department must hold a hearing for each tenement at which the owner could present his case. The plea was bolstered by a long list of decisions affirming the rights of property.

In their deliberations, the justices were swayed more by

advances in sanitation than by the sanctity of profit. Scientists said people are cleaner and healthier when they do not have to carry all their water up four or five flights of stairs. Plumbing had reached such a stage of technological development that pipes could now be installed in every city home. So the justices fell back on a common law concept first enunciated in the Supreme Court by John Marshall. Their inherent police power authorizes governments to modify constitutional prohibitions in the interest of the health and welfare of citizens.

"Laws and regulations of a police nature, though they may disturb the enjoyment of individual rights, are not unconstitutional, though no provision is made for compensation for such disturbance," the 1895 decision by Justice Rufus W. Peckham reads. "They do not appropriate private property for public use, but simply regulate enjoyment by the owner. If he suffer injury . . . in the theory of the laws he is compensated for it by sharing in the general benefits which the regulations are intended and calculated to secure."

Health Department v. Trinity Church represents only part of the Law that enables government to set standards for technological advances. But such advances are fast, and the pace of regulatory legislation is slow. By the time a statute is passed, the damage may be done. To meet such contingencies, Law may rely on other resources than the lawmakers, chiefly a long memory and a revolutionary spirit that overturns doctrines tenaciously held.

The long memory comes into play when an ancient statute or precedent, ignored or forgotten for years, is dredged up to remedy a modern wrong. Such a legal resurrection took place in 1970 when the country was becoming unhappily aware that unpleasant or dangerous consequences may flow from some industrial processes highly regarded for their contributions to the comforts and ease of life.

An Ontario university student set off this call for Law to

restrain technology in March when he discovered that substantially larger amounts of mercury than human beings can safely eat had accumulated in wall-eyed pike caught in Lake St. Clair, which is partly in Michigan and partly in Canada. The safe level of mercury in fish to be consumed by people has been put at one-half part per million. More than that can build up in the human system with disastrous effects on the brain, kidneys, and liver. Some of the St. Clair pike had as much as seven parts per million. It turned out that a single chemical plant was discharging 200 pounds of mercury a day into the St. Clair River, which flows into the lake. Within weeks, water and the fish caught in it were being analyzed for mercury all over the United States and Canada. Many were badly contaminated, not always by mercury. Fisheries were closed, water declared unsafe to drink.

Since mercury does not occur in water naturally, the hunt was on for culprits. The stuff is a waste from a great variety of manufacturing processes—chemicals, paper, electric batteries, and many more. In the absence of any general alarm, hundreds of factories simply let the mercury run off with other waste into the nearest stream or lake. This has been the standard procedure for disposing of refuse since the industrial revolution and before. Suddenly the special hazards of mercury sharpened a growing public sentiment that it was high time we improve standard waste-disposal procedures.

The initial impulse of those who wanted to sue the polluters was to rely on the Federal Water Pollution Control Act of 1966, one of the first fruits of growing national concern over technology's threat to the environment. But after a second look, impatient conservationists dismissed this statute as a fine example of Law's leaning toward leisurely diagnosis while the patient dies. The most rapid procedure that the act permitted was for the government to serve an abatement notice on an offender and hold a hearing. If the hearing revealed that materials harmful to humans, other animals, or plants were being dumped into any navigable waters in the United States, the polluter must be allowed 180 days to mend his ways. Only after a failure to do so could he be taken to court.

Government lawyers looked for a speedier remedy. (An often quoted but not so frequently observed dictum of Law is that justice delayed is justice denied.) They found what they were looking for in an almost forgotten Refuse Act of 1899, which would have a hard time running the gantlet of industrial lobbies in Washington today. This statute forbids anyone who does not have a permit from the Army Corps of Engineers to dump any refuse, except ordinary sewage or the runoff from streets, into streams, lakes, or the sea, under penalty of imprisonment up to a year and fines up to $2,500 a day. Nothing is said about abatement hearings or 180-day delays. As an incentive to enforcement, the act allows an informer half the fine. However, this clause was a well-kept secret, and no one had ever demanded compliance with the permit requirements.

Within a matter of weeks after the mercury disclosures, the machinery of Law began to move not only in cases involving mercury but all sorts of other water pollution by industries. Representatives Michael Harrington of Massachusetts and Henry Reuss of Wisconsin listed some 300 such violators in their states alone. The Corps of Engineers began inspections. Conservation groups accused hundreds of factories in many states—so many that the Department of Justice instructed United States attorneys, the Federal prosecutors, to use the Refuse Act only when dumping occurred infrequently through accident or carelessness. Other polluters, said the Department, should be left to the mercies of the Water Quality Administration, created by the 1966 Act. Yet Congress had stipulated that the 1966 measure was not to supersede the Refuse Act. Within a few days, public outcry and a request from the Interior Department for prosecution of eight large companies led Justice to modify the instructions. The eight companies were said to be dumping mercury in dangerous amounts into waters from

Puget Sound to the Penobscot River, including the Columbia, Delaware, Niagara, and Tennessee Rivers.

By July, the Refuse Act of 1899 was clearly alive and well. In hundreds, perhaps thousands of manufacturing establishments, technicians were being ordered to devise ways to clean up effluents. The first case settled in court was one of Law's rarely speedy moves. The Washburn Wire Company of New York City was indicted on Octorber 21 on fifty counts after inspectors for the Army Engineers found it had been dumping without a permit into one of the dirtiest of all waterways, the Harlem River. Eight days later, the company pleaded guilty before a Federal judge, Constance Motley Baker, who, as a woman and a black, had been known to express concern for the deterioration of urban environments. She levied the maximum fine, $2,500, for each of the fifty violations but suspended payment because the company was spending a good deal more than that for settling basins to remove polluting metals from water before it is released into the river.

Other companies were taking similar steps. Still others were issuing statements to the effect that some pollution is inevitable in the technological age in which we live if we want to maintain all our automobiles, electrical equipment, fancy packaging, and other status symbols of the affluent society. Obviously Law was driving more and more scientifically trained men and women to a search for techniques to undo the damage caused by the machines that other scientifically trained men and women had devised.

Profound study of Law is more likely to stimulate reverence for the status quo than fervor for sudden change. Yet good lawyers do become thorough revolutionaries; they have been in the forefront of all national revolutions. And when one of them makes his revolution in law, even the idols created by Science may be brought low. If he is strategically placed, he can do it singlehanded.

Benjamin Nathan Cardozo was such a lawyer. As the Chief Judge of New York State's highest court, destined for distinguished service on the Supreme Court in Washington, he spoke from the vantage point of one of the country's most respected tribunals. Between 1913 and 1916, by which time he was 46 years old, he had gone from the lowest state court to the top of the highest, and in the process completely reversed his legal philosophy. When he was in private practice, he once explained, he looked only for precedents to support his case because he was certain that all judges followed such authorities inexorably.

"I was not much concerned whether it was right if I was sure that it was pertinent," he said.

As a judge, he saw things differently. As advocate, he could ignore everything but the narrow interests of his client. As arbiter, he began to think in terms of a dynamic system of law that, as he put it, "is adjusted to the ends which law should serve." As a lawyer, he had argued that any change should come from the legislature in the form of specific statutes making specific reforms. On the bench, he still thought this desirable but added that since legislators are only amateurs and judges are professionals, the more expert gentlemen inevitably create new law to fit modern innovations.

"Decisions . . . unrelated to present-day realities ought not to be permitted to prescribe a rule of life," he wrote in *The Growth of the Law,* and: "The judge interprets the social experience and gives effect to it in law, but in so doing he helps to form and modify the conscience he interprets. Discovery and creation react upon each other."

Such reflections led him directly to his revolutionary ideas, and during his first year as Chief Judge, 1916, he got his chance to put them into effect. As usual, the Revolution in Law was churned out while society was undergoing a massive and fundamental change, this one caused by the emergence of the automobile as a means of mass transportation. Only a few years earlier, the public's main concern had been that these monstrous toys scared horses. Amusement rather than alarm was inspired by such incidents as a chase in Cincinnati in 1907 when a policeman on a bicycle overtook a car driven by Miss Helen Taft, waved her to the curb, and gave her a ticket for speeding—fine $10. By 1916, however, the Model T Ford was outselling every other car on the market. The number of motor vehicles on the still mostly miserable roads was in the millions.

The automobile's accident rate was as impressive as its sales. The so-called "Ford fracture," a wrist broken when the engine backfired while a man was cranking it (few women had the strength) was being eliminated by Charles Kettering's self-starter. But crashes due to faulty steering gears, brakes that did not hold, or engine failures kept the toll rising. For a judge like Cardozo, who spoke of using creative imagination in one's approach to Law, this represented a challenge.

The challenge had to be met when one of the typical automobile liability cases that already were cluttering lower-court calendars reached Cardozo's august tribunal. *MacPherson v. Buick Motor Company* attracted little attention because, on the face of it, the only interesting feature was MacPherson's effrontery in suing the maker instead of the dealer. At this time, a long line of precedents held that you could not haul into court people with whom you never had any dealings. If you had a complaint about a product, you directed it to the man or company from whom you purchased it. Since the manufacturer sold no cars directly to consumers, MacPherson could hardly bring an action against Buick. Or so Buick contended.

The mishap that triggered a revolution was so common that few newspapers would report it. MacPherson, driving a 1914 Buick, was painfully injured when the wooden spokes of a wheel broke. Experts who examined the wreckage testified that a latent defect was responsible, and a jury awarded MacPherson appropriate damages. The company appealed on the basis of both their lack of any dealings with the car owner and an ancient legal maxim expressed in Latin, as many are, *caveat emptor,* "let the buyer beware."

For generations this had served to dismiss claims by people who complained that an improperly or unsafely made product had maimed them or damaged their property. Before they could collect, they had to prove that the seller knew of the fault or knew that the goods he sold were harmful or dangerous. The flaw in the Buick's wheel was detected only after it broke. The company's counsel pointed out that it was up to the buyer of a motor car to spot defects before he paid for it, just as he had to do for any other purchase. The lawyers cited a virtual catalogue of decisions that supported this position.

Cardozo's revolution reversed this well-known doctrine. It may have served in the remote past when anything a man bought was so simply constructed that he could reasonably be expected to detect any flaws. But by 1916, the complexity of many ordinary articles of commerce was so great that hardly anyone could understand the mechanism, let alone judge the quality. Cardozo held that under these conditions *caveat emptor* was unrealistic and therefore could no longer be considered good law. Furthermore, a manufacturer whose products are offered to the public assumes an obligation. He guarantees, in effect, that what he sells is free from avoidable defects. This principle holds for any area, regardless of middlemen, so MacPherson had a perfect right to go to the source of the damage. The jury's verdict stood.

The decision implied a certain negligence on Buick's part in not setting up proper inspection procedures. But it is by no means certain that vigilance is always protection. During the rest of his term as Chief Judge, Cardozo's court carried the case against *caveat emptor* two steps further.

The first step was *Rinaldi v. the Mohican Company,* involving the sale of pork that gave the purchaser trichinosis. The company denied liability on the ground that no method of inspection then known could have revealed this taint. Therefore, no implication of negligence could stand. The court agreed that this was true, but ruled that Mohican must pay for Rinaldi's illness anyway. In patronizing the company, he had in effect relied upon its skill and judgment since it was in a better position than he to know about meat. Neither was at fault, but the company, better able to stand the cost than the customer, must bear the responsibility.

Cardozo's next step, taken in 1931, the year before he left New York to fill Oliver Wendell Holmes's place on the Supreme Court, completed his revolution. He did it with a pin and a loaf of bread. The juxtaposition of these homely items, the pin inside the bread, brought them to the New York Court of Appeals under the title of *Ryan v. Progressive Grocery Stores.* Mrs. Ryan had asked a clerk at one of the defendant's chain stores for a loaf of Ward's bread, and when her husband bit into a slice, the pin pierced his mouth. He demanded damages. The loaf, of course, had been sealed in its package at the bakery; no one at Progressive Grocery Stores had touched it except to transfer it from a truck to the shelf and from the shelf to Mrs. Ryan's shopping bag.

The court's ruling was complicated by a new Personal Property Law passed since *Buick* and *Mohican.* This embodied what might be called *caveat vendor,* "let the seller beware," with reservations. It set forth even more clearly than Cardozo had done that if a buyer asks for any product by its generic name, as bread or beer or an electric toaster, he is in effect relying upon the seller's expertise to supply an item that is fit for its purpose. By the act of handing it over, the seller guarantees that the thing is "of merchantable quality." If this warranty fails, he is liable. But, the statute continued, if the buyer asks for the product by its brand name, the seller does not imply anything, and so gives no warranty.

Lawyers for Progressive Grocery Stores asserted that in asking for Ward's bread by name, Mrs. Ryan was not relying upon the clerk's knowledge, so she received no warranty that the loaf was fit to eat. They also said that the grocer was justified in supposing that a company that turned out thousands of loaves every day, with nary a pin in the lot, furnished bread "of merchantable quality." As a last resort, counsel suggested that even if their client was liable, it could only be for the value of the defective loaf—then 5 cents.

Cardozo's opinion was unusually recondite and circuitously reasoned, with elaborate references to solutions of similar problems by other courts. But his key points are straightforward and clearly stated. A doctrine of *caveat vendor* should not exclude liability for those who have won enough public confidence that people ask for their products by brand name. Presumably the legislature was mistaken. So brushing aside the theory that in these cases no fitness is implied, he concentrated on the thesis that a merchant or manufacturer who purveys goods to the public is responsible for them. He ruled that "loaves baked with pins in them are not of merchantable quality," and a little later, "the law casts the burden on the seller." You could hardly repeal *caveat emptor* more explicitly.

Cardozo's revolutionary philosophy was rooted in his belief that the ordinary citizen is no match in technical knowledge and understanding for operators of the new devices and processes that Science pours forth at an accelerating pace. He agreed with impassioned corporation counsel that *caveat vendor* might be unfair to men who were guiltless of wrongdoing. But he offered those unfortunates no relief.

"The burden may be heavy," he wrote in ordering the grocer to pay Ryan. "It is one of the hazards of the business."

This chapter's three glimpses of Law in action hardly exhaust either her variety in dealing with the problems Science raises or the multiplying novelty of those problems. Law has other devices up the voluminous sleeve of her robe. It is by no means certain that she can shake them out in time to regulate the technology that has overtaken us already, let alone the Janus-like marvels that loom over our immediate future, promising us health and wealth and ease on one hand, and on the other threatening us with deterioration and disaster. This is the dilemma that comes next.

Part One

LAW IN SPACE

2 | Above the Air

When Russia's Sputnik opened the door to the moon and the planets, the prospect that Law would be able to keep up with what has been called "rampant technology" seemed remote. Her usage and precedents, based on exploration of the earth and the uses men made of the oceans, were pitifully inadequate. Such Law as was relevant had been evolved by a small group of maritime nations for their own benefit and arrogantly imposed upon the rest of the world. Now neither the backward nations nor the so-called advanced ones were likely to tolerate the extension of such rules into outer space.

Under the old code, any new territory belonged to the country that hired the discoverer or claimed him as a citizen, provided that the territory was occupied "effectively." This was a serviceably vague expression that left plenty of room for controversy through diplomacy or arms. On earth, the disputes were sometimes susceptible to resolution by Law. But usually it was only after a war or secret negotiations or both that Law entered the picture by formally registering the settlement in the legal documents known as treaties.

The system worked so long as the small group of maritime nations had the power to parcel out the continents among themselves. Thus the Pope divided the Western Hemisphere between Spain and Portugal. England, France and the Netherlands seized their share a little later. All five fought and bargained among themselves for their "rights" to the New World while Sweden, Denmark and Russia unobtrusively picked up bits and pieces.

By the time of Sputnik, this system already was outmoded on earth. The great colonial empires had collapsed and disintegrated into separate states, and the prospect of space exploration conducted under the rules prevailing in the time of Columbus, Magellan, Henry Hudson and Sir Walter Raleigh appealed to no one.

A little more applicable to travel in space is the international law developed over centuries to regulate the passage of ships and airplanes over water and through air that is claimed by no single nation. The universally accepted principle that all men have an equal right of free passage on the high seas is subject only to some agreed-upon regulations to keep them from bumping into each other or plundering each other. This principle can be taken over for travelers in space. So can the rule that the nation in whose name a vessel is registered retains jurisdiction over it while it is on the ocean or in flight.

Other problems that will not fit into the law of the sea and air can easily be envisaged. Piracy, for example, was suppressed, except for isolated instances, after many centuries when the maritime powers finally agreed that it was a universal crime. But the same acceptance of such a rule is lacking in the air, let alone in space. The aerial version, hijacking, is at the same stage piracy was during the reign of Queen Elizabeth I, when it was condoned if committed against ships of an unfriendly country. As Englishmen admired what Spain considered the piracy of Sir Francis Drake, Arabs applaud Palestine guerrilla hijackers. Aerial pirates on one side of the iron curtain are not punished on the other.

To allow such a legal situation to prevail in space could provoke intolerable conflicts. In addition, other international problems present themselves more insistently than those that obviously parallel our experience in aviation. Men's activities in space, once they escalate to massive proportions, may well have damaging effects on land or in the atmosphere that would make hijacking appear no more serious than a childish prank. If space ships discharge a fraction of the wastes of ocean-going liners, the effect might be a profound alteration in the radiation reaching earth from the sun. Our planet could become uninhabitable through this interference with nature before the rest of us bring about the same result with pollution generated on the ground.

Then, too, a potential source of conflict between nations is espionage. Surveillance from miles up can be far more revealing than from miles out at sea. Further knowledge of the interaction of man and space may disclose other dangers. Only Law can avert the disasters they threaten, and fortunately she has responded with unaccustomed alacrity.

Within a year after the first man-made satellite went into orbit, talks about supranational control of men in space began at the United Nations. Usually Law has moved at about the pace of molasses in January while Science has been dashing ahead with something approaching the speed of light. But before the actual landing of men on the moon, a substantial body of space law had been written and agreed upon. Of course, it remains to be seen whether it will be enforced.

The first step was a resolution adopted unanimously by the United Nations General Assembly to keep the peace in space. This forbade the launching of any satellite that carried weapons of mass destruction or the installation of such weapons "on celestial bodies." The text specifically mentioned nuclear arms. Months later the United Nations Committee on the Peaceful Uses of Outer Space adopted what it called a Declaration of Legal Principles. This asserted the right of all to explore outer space and denied the right of any to claim exclusive jurisdiction anywhere. Some basic provisions were included for making nations responsible for what they do, for mutual consultation, and for payment of damages.

This declaration was formalized and expanded in 1967 in a document with a mouth-filling title—The Treaty on Principles Governing the Activities of States in the Exploration and Use of Outer Space, Including the Moon and Other Celestial Bodies. It was duly ratified not only by the United States and the Soviet Union, the two countries with space programs that matter, but by most of the rest of the world and all nations with a space potential except China. This was followed a year later by an only slightly less important Agreement on the Rescue of Astronauts and the Return of Objects Launched into Outer Space.

Among them, these documents may very well prove a great legal leap forward, corresponding to those of Newton, Freud and Einstein in Science. Such leaps in Law can replace the tiny, timid steps by which our legal system usually moves.

On the face of it, the Outer Space Treaty does represent such a leap and one that could have repercussions on earth. Stretching the human mind to new limits often carries the fresh idea over into areas other than that toward which it was originally directed. Law that can create a harmony of nations in space might teach the nations subject to it how to apply the same rules for peace on earth.

The treaty became the law of the United States on October 10, 1967, taking precedence in the legal hierarchy ahead of acts of Congress and after the Constitution. It commits this country, and all the other signatories, of course, to abide by these rules:

1. Any activities on any celestial body will be conducted "in the interest of maintaining international peace and security and promoting international cooperation and understanding." Nowhere, either on a celestial body or a man-made satellite, will any nuclear or other weapons of mass destruction be placed, whether for testing or any other purpose.

2. The United Nations, the public, and the international scientific community shall be advised of the nature, operations, location, and results of all space activities. Inspections may be made by any state that so desires, either by direct aerial observation or by monitoring communications.

3. All states may freely explore and use all of outer space and the celestial bodies, but none may appropriate any special rights. Rather, all exploration and use shall be "for the benefit and in the interest of all nations irrespective of economic or scientific development and shall be the province of all mankind."

4. All space studies shall be carried out with care to avoid contamination or other danger to the environment of either a celestial body or earth.

5. If any private, nongovernmental activities are undertaken in space, the government of the country where they originate is required both to authorize and supervise them.

The American investment in satellite telecommunications, known as Comsat, already comes under that last clause. Other ventures that will be similarly covered impend. By the middle of 1970, Pan American Airlines had taken 70,000 reservations for lunar trips that it projected for an admittedly indefinite future. A round-trip ticket was expected to cost about $14,000. Nothing was said of one-way tickets.

So far, space law has been reasonably well observed; at least no complaints or charges of violations have been voiced. Both the United States and Russia make the results of their explorations known promptly. The United States delivers an annual report of its activities to the Secretary General of the United Nations, and special interim reports on scientific matters. Neither Russia nor the United States has advanced any claims to special rights of any kind on the strength of their pioneer enterprises on the moon or elsewhere in space. The principle that one country's research should not interfere with another's was not always observed before the legal restraints were formulated. When the United States decided to put a mass of tiny copper filaments into orbit as part of a 1965 communications experiment, all the other nations involved in space were consulted beforehand. They objected that the filaments might interfere with radio transmission or the space observations of others. When the United States refuted this, they still protested against the plan on the ground that it might be potentially dangerous. But the experiment was conducted anyway, although it was not repeated. On another occasion, before the Test Ban Treaty of 1963, the United States carried out a series of high-altitude nuclear explosions over international protests. The objection to these was, in addition to the radiation menace present in all nuclear explosions, possible damage to the Van Allen Belt, the bands of radiation that surround the earth in the upper atmosphere. Any alteration might affect radio transmission and have other unpredictable consequences.

It remains to be seen whether this leap into peaceful coexistence of nations in outer space can survive the tests of the future. As the satellites, space platforms, and space vehicles increase in number, inconvenient or onerous traffic rules may become necessary. Advantages not yet foreseen may accrue to a nation that controls a given area on the moon. The fears of one nation or group of nations that another has become a deadly danger may lead to a warlike posture in which leaders rationalize that armed satellites in space are an urgent security need. In anticipation of that day, Law may seek to develop enforcement machinery to hold the treaty signatories to their pledged word.

The record of nations in observing the international law embodied in such documents is not encouraging. Even the United States has been a party to solemn compacts by which it (and others, of course) renounced war as an instrument of national policy in the most explicit terms. Yet this country has been engaged in war most of the time since ratification. The substitutes for war that this body of international law envisaged proved ineffective whenever some government felt itself or its people pinched or endangered. And other gaps have been left for the law of space to fill.

One of the first and seemingly simplest questions to be solved is where outer space begins. The treaty does not offer a definition. This was not an oversight but recognition of the fact that nations are jealous of anything they own, even air or empty space above the air, and reluctant to give up control. Of course, everyone agrees there has to be a limit, just as there is to the amount of ocean a country can take over as its territorial waters. At sea, the community of nations never has reached an agreement, the range of claims asserted and enforced being from three to two hundred miles, with a majority settling for twelve. No greater unanimity has been achieved on air rights, even among citizens of the same country. Some Americans have proposed a boundary to the national air at the theoretical limit of the flight of ordinary aircraft, which is about fifty miles. Above that, the air is believed to be too thin to support conventional planes. Other experts argue that some national control should be retained up to three hundred miles. Law's first practical step in space may well be its solution of this problem. Or it may more speedily be faced with a question arising from the treaty that covers objects and people who return to earth in another country than the one that launched them.

Astronauts themselves have been invested with the status of diplomats who are not subject to detention by any foreign country. As popular heroes, they would hardly need this protection now. But as space travel becomes more common, travelers could be intolerably harassed if Law remained what it was before the 1967 treaty. Then any human visitor from outer space could be treated as a spy. Now his whereabouts must be announced publicly, and his return to his own country is guaranteed.

Since most of the present exploration is carried on by means of unmanned spacecraft, the treaty was concerned with the delivery to the original owners of instruments and records that might go astray somewhere on earth or on the future space platforms of another country. It was provided, therefore, that any nation finding such an object is obliged to inform the country of origin promptly and also inform the United Nations. If the country of origin wants it, the finding country must send it back at the expense of the country of origin. However, if the object "is of a hazardous or deleterious nature," the finding country may call upon those who launched it "to eliminate possible danger or harm," again at the launcher's expense.

Law, and especially that embodied in treaties, is seldom so clear that only one interpretation of any set of circumstances is possible. Precise meanings develop when the words are subjected to hard decisions in specific instances, either by governments or courts. The Outer Space Treaty forbids placing weapons in orbit. But legal authorities do not agree as to whether that includes partial orbit. The treaty itself spells out no specific procedures for resolving the issue if two countries disagree. The situation could be further complicated if a weapon carrier in partial orbit that caused such a dispute came down in the territory of a third country. The obligation of this country to return it to the land of its origin might be argued either under the terms of the Outer Space Treaty or the provisions of the later return agreement for handling dangerous objects.

It is quite conceivable that many other words and phrases will be subject to disputes. Exactly what is meant by a "space object" could be litigated in great detail. The term was chosen during the drafting of the treaty only after "space vehicle" was rejected as too exclusive. But whether everything coming back from space is included, such as a traveler's luggage or only parts and instruments that are essential to the operation of a space craft or laboratory, remains to be decided. Similar judgments will be made as to when an object is "found," when it is "impracticable" to arrange its return, where "territorial limits" begin and end, what constitutes adequate "identification," what is in fact "contamination," what is "hazardous," and what are the rights and protection due to people who may get in the way of such objects or be damaged by them either bodily or in their property. Not even hinted at is crime in space and who has jurisdiction over it—not surprising since it has been impossible to settle on rules of law to cover such crimes in the air as hijacking.

No doubt the eminent international jurists who will have to make these interpretations will seek inspiration from the twistings and turnings by which technology's earlier innovations in transportation changed Law in their day. Railroads, then automobiles, and finally airplanes raised legal issues as novel and in some ways more immediately pressing than Sputnik and Apollo 11. The solutions reached in this country are instructive, sometimes for their wisdom and sometimes as examples to be avoided.

Of the three, railroads were the most obviously objectionable to adjoining property owners, especially when the property was next to a busy railroad yard. Today such property would hardly be used for any human activity that was very adversely affected by noise, dirt, or vibration. But in their early days, railroads were built with little consideration for neighboring homeowners, farmers or businesses. Householders, farmers and merchants sued when the situation became intolerable. Law floundered for some time among the claims of compensation for sleepless nights and grimy wash, aborted cows and noise-crazed chickens, lost trade and ruined stocks of goods. Eventually, Law settled on a theory that the entire population benefited so much from improved transportation that the losses and discomforts of individuals could be ignored or written off as the unfortunate but inevitable price of progress, a sort of tax imposed upon the victims. They were supposed to be sharers in the fruits of rail transportation, and that was their compensation.

The automobile brought some of the objectionable qualities associated with railroads into pleasant neighborhoods uncontaminated by tracks. The main damage at first was scared horses; the roar and fumes of traffic on highways suddenly erupting in front of a man's house came later. In both cases, Law applied the rule she had developed for the railroads. A key decision was made by New York's highest court in 1900 in *Neher v. West*. Neher was a horseman injured when the West automobile frightened his mount. The judges held that progress in motoring and the public convenience resulting therefrom had reached the point where the liability imposed upon a mere toy or experiment was no longer reasonable. Once it might have been the motorist's obligation to keep away from horses. Now horses must get used to cars. In order to collect damages, Neher would have to prove that West had been operating his vehicle recklessly or negligently. All the evidence at the trial indicated that he had driven carefully. Again the general benefits of the new means of transportation were held to outweigh the harm to individuals.

These rules were well within the legal boundaries settled over the centuries. But Law took another look at the basic principles when people began complaining about airplanes. Chiefly they objected to the noise as planes scooted low over their heads. In the beginning, they might have been protected by the rights inherent in their ownership of land, for, according to the United States Civil Code of 1910, this "extends downward and upwards indefinitely." But aviation could not exist if it had to get a permit from every proprietor for the use of his air. So in 1926, Congress simply confiscated the right of transit through all air and gave everyone permission to fly through it freely. Furthermore, Congress did not pay anyone a cent for the property so summarily requisitioned. No doubt the members conceded that a man might own a column of air reaching to infinity, but it was valueless to him.

Under the new Act, the right to fly anywhere was subject to navigation regulations of the Civil Aeronautics Authority. These rules could keep aircraft from flying so low as to be unbearable except when they were landing and taking off. Whether in these circumstances they were to be put in the legal category of locomotives and automobiles was uncertain until the combination of a world war and a litigious chicken farmer led the Supreme Court to take a hard look at the problem.

The time was 1942, only a few months after Pearl Harbor, and the United States was expanding the Air Forces feverishly. The new planes needed air fields, and in this emergency the Army leased a little-used municipal airport at Greensboro, North Carolina. In May, big bombers and transports began to use the field, and in June they were arriving and departing all through the day and night. From one runway, the "safe glide angle" for takeoff and landing took them exactly 67 feet above the roof of Thomas and Tinie Causby's house. The Causbys made a living from their chicken farm of some two and three-quarters acres that adjoined the airport. Within a few months, their chickens had been scared to death, killed as they dashed themselves against walls and fences, and Thomas and Tinie were nervous wrecks from loss of sleep and worry. They sued the United States, claiming that the government had in effect confiscated their farm for war purposes and should pay a fair price for it. The government replied that the Army planes were flying according to the regulations through air that was free for the use of all, and the Causbys were in the same fix as if they lived next to a railroad.

The Causby claim was based on the Fifth Amendment's last clause, "nor shall private property be taken for public use, without just compensation." Lawyers for the Causbys argued that when Congress confiscated the air for purposes of aviation it did not mean *all* the air. They said their clients still owned what was immediately over the house and grounds, at least up to a level where trespass in it seriously inconvenienced the occupants. Alternatively, counsel proposed, the constant noisy flights had much diminished the value of the farm itself, the solid land, and was therefore a partial "taking" within the meaning of the Fifth Amendment. Government attorneys replied that this would be true only if the land became fit for nothing and the house completely uninhabitable. As to ownership of any air, surely Congress meant to make public that which was needed for getting up and down as well as that needed for level flight.

The merits of the case are not as obvious to judges as they may seem to laymen. *United States v. Causby* wound its way through the Court of Claims, the U.S. Court of Appeals, and the Supreme Court without gaining a unanimous decision in any of the three. However, in all three the Causbys won a majority. The Court of Claims awarded them $2,000 over the objection of one member. The other two judges were impressed by a ruling of the Georgia Supreme Court in 1942 that while a properly run airport might be in the same privileged position as a nuisance as the railroads, to be properly run it had to have enough land for planes to clear the neighbors' houses with more than a few feet to spare. In this case, known in the books as *Kersey v. City of Atlanta,* the "safe glide angle" put aircraft only 30 feet over the Kersey home. This fit the circumstances in Greensboro, said the claims judges, and the Court of Appeals concurred, also with one dissent. The Supreme Court confirmed the award by six to two. The opinion set *Causby* apart from railroad cases on the ground that a man still owns "at least as much of the space above the ground as he can use in connection with the land" whereas he had no share in the ownership of land used by locomotives or automobiles.

One suspects that space law will more likely be a spin-off from aviation precedents than from other transportation principles. It will also create its own. Although this whole province of Law will be founded upon a leap of the human mind away from traditional wisdom, those who achieve the leap will assure us of just the opposite. They will assert with all solemnity, and no doubt in good faith, that their innovation always was the law and is simply being perfected and brought into harmony

with new conditions. Lawyers and judges will point with satisfaction to pertinent precedents in the old railroad or automobile cases, even if they have to stretch the meaning a bit.
But this does no harm. In fact, it adds somewhat to the apparent stability of Law.

Despite the durable impression and the ultimate result, the
development probably will be uncertain, unpredictable in detail. Yet, because it remains Law, basic principles will still apply. One of these is that the ultimate solution will be decided
by the people, either through their demand for a specific conclusion or by their indifference to results. In the latter case,
lawyers and diplomats will make the decisions. Either way, the
rule eventually worked out will achieve, as all Law must, some
balance between the risks that any human activity entails.
Whatever the final outcome, one man's gains will be another's
loss unless we forswear the fruits of experimenting with the
unknown because we fear its dangers. Law seeks to balance
these risks, but neither Law nor Science can provide sufficient
knowledge to be sure the balance is perfect. The goal of both is
certainly based on logic and experience, but as Oliver Wendell
Holmes once explained:

"The language of judicial decision is mainly the language
of logic, and the logical method and form flatter that longing
for certainty and repose which is in every human mind. But
certainty generally is illusion, and repose is not the destiny of
man."

Law can come only so close to the great objective as to
give guidelines firm enough that men need not guess themselves into jail and nations not guess themselvess into a war.
The line between the tolerable risk and intolerable recklessness
may be very fine. The first encourages the search for beneficial
technological discoveries. The second poses the danger of disasters far greater than the potential gains. Both benefits and
dangers become more obvious as one examines some of the
specific possibilities of man's activities in space.

3 | The Uses of Space

Men whose business is foretelling the future are very chary of applying the word "impossible" to any technological dream, no matter how far out. They also are aware that the potential capacities of many machines and processes already in use are virtually limitless. The soothsayers of Science were not always so cautious in proclaiming their modern equivalent of Delphian prophecy. In 1937, a group of the most eminent of them, leading physical and social scientists appointed and financed by the Federal government, issued a report entitled "Technological Trends and National Policy." In it, they undertook to assess the unprecedented rate at which scientific discoveries had been applied in the first third of the 20th century and to calculate likely directions and accomplishments for the next third.

One of the report's major sections dealt with aviation, which could be more completely reviewed than most subjects because heavier-than-air machines were entirely a product of the period being studied. So far as the speed of flight was concerned, said the distinguished authorities, the peak had been reached. By this time, airplanes already had flown at 300 miles an hour. Clearly nothing faster could be achieved. Future aviation development would be confined to improvements in safety and comfort.

40

The scientists' crystal ball of 1937 also failed to appreciate the budding important technological changes that would be among the notable achievements of the second third of the century. Some of these already were foreshadowed by the mathematicians and physicists of the day. But the trends discussed in the report made no mention of the jet engine that would make 1937 air speeds seem like those of ox carts, nor of atomic fission and nuclear energy, nor of the new fields opened by radar, nor of the mechanical brain then portrayed in science fiction and later brought to reality as a computer. Finally, the published documents contained no hint of man's exploration of outer space.

A third of a century after this understandable lapse by some of the country's best scientific minds, the practical uses of space in the service of men seem to be as extensive as the furthest reaches of the human imagination. Spacecraft, not necessarily limited to the speed of light, may well put us in regular communication with planets and rational beings far beyond the boundaries of our own solar system. Emigration to some other universe may become humanity's escape from an irreparably polluted earth. Science may lead man rapidly to such an adaptation as evolution achieved slowly. That one began when the first animal crawling out of the sea managed to convert its gills into a mechanism for breathing air. The new humans may well find themselves adjusting to at least as great a change.

What role Law would play in such a technologically advanced world has already concerned a few thinkers. It has been suggested that we might have to jettison our legal concepts of property, personal rights, and collective responsibility in favor of quite different principles. Andrew G. Haley, a scientist as well as a lawyer, has suggested that the future will require a broader and more equitable system of justice than the one we now use, even if we always lived up to the highest professions of our present code. He sees this new system as being beyond law as we know it, and he coined for it the term "megalaw." He thought it might include, for example, a higher ethic than what is perhaps the highest ever voiced on earth—Jesus' Golden Rule of doing unto others as you would have them do unto you. In a remote universe peopled by beings whose lives have been governed by completely different standards and traditions than any humanity has ever known, we might have to "do unto others as they want to be done by," and not only profess it as an ideal but incorporate it into Law. In other words, Science might plunge us into situations where man's arrogant assumption that he always knows best, not only what is good for his fellows but for other creatures, too, would have to be abandoned. In its place, this outer-space evolution would create in him an unaccustomed humility as a condition of survival, not just a moral imperative.

These speculations presuppose a greater acceptance of international law than peaceful exploration of space has so far required. Some hints at the problems and prospects may be found in the uses of space that are actually in effect. Of these, the most firmly established is communication by satellite, first envisioned in a science-fiction piece by Arthur C. Clarke in 1945. Television is the best known beneficiary at the moment, but data and facsimile transmission, radio and picturephones are among already practicable features too.

Law regulates these communications internationally through multination agreement, although so far without the inclusion of a great many, such as Russia. Inside the United States, the regulatory agency is the Federal Communications Commission. Within the satellite system, of which this country is the dominant partner, the general setup is not unlike the domestic telephone and telegraph networks—a private corporation operating under government regulation. The overall body was formed in July 1964, when nineteen nations joined in the International Telecommunications Satellite Consortium (mercifully shortened to Intelsat) under an agreement that assured the United States member of the consortium at least 50.5 percent of the stock no matter how many additional countries were admitted. The American shares are held by a domestic company chartered by the government for the purpose, Communications Satellite Corporation (Comsat). It started out with 61 percent of the shares, reduced to 55 percent after six years, by which time the total membership had grown to seventy-nine countries. Under a 1971 agreement, the United States is slated to become a minority stockholder. When the shares were issued, there was no lack of buyers at $45 a share, and Comsat proved almost immune to the 1969–70 stock market slump. The shares almost doubled in value.

The justification for the United States financial control of Intelsat was that most of the money and most of the research that the participants put into this aspect of space technology was American. In 1971, however, the Administration was considering reduction of the United States interest to much less than half because others use the facilities more. Of course, Russia did not join, and the machinery of international law has not yet worked out a formula within which both the major space powers could be accommodated harmoniously for the joint use of communications satellites.

Intelsat was not long in reaching its operating phase. The first Early Bird satellite was launched in 1965. It was able to transmit through 240 circuits; its best-known uses were in commercial television. The *Bulletin of Atomic Scientists* somewhat bitterly complained that this really spectacular technological advance was being devoted to "pictures of royal weddings, sports events, funeral processions, street demonstrations, and assorted public violence." This is a common criticism of television in general, and since Comsat is an integral part of our overall communications network, it is governed by much the same principles. However, it is worth noting that programs devoted to more learned or formally educational subjects than the *Bulletin* mentioned have been broadcast by satellite, and the proportion of news and comment on public affairs is much greater than will be found on the conventionally transmitted hours of any commercial station.

Furthermore, the capacity of Intelsat has been greatly increased. By 1972, it had four satellites, two about 22,000 miles up over the Atlantic, and one each over the Pacific and Indian oceans, and the number of circuits had risen to 1,200. By the time this is published, Intelsat expects to have 9,600 circuits. The cost of operating each will have been brought down from the $20,000 a year of 1965 to something in the neighborhood of $500. This will begin to be competitive with earthbound means of communication between continents, although coaxial cables now in use on land carry up to 30,000 circuits at once and in a few years should have triple that capacity.

Law in its present state leaves some serious gaps in safeguarding people from the abuses of satellite communication. Those who think commercial television has failed them in the areas of news and education will seek a change in the rules for Intelsat. Those who think the present system gives people what they want and is therefore satisfactory accept the rules as they are.

More immediately, the new communications expose a need for change in the laws of obscenity, libel, slander, privacy, copyright, and unfair competition. As long as satellite broadcasts are filtered through the present networks, which can be held liable under law, the problem remains manageable. But when the viewer can tune in directly to the source of a satellite broadcast, the situation will pose some new difficulties.

Law will then have to decide whose standards of good taste and criticism of public officials or private persons are to prevail. The source may be in a country that has no laws against obscenity or punishes severely even the mildest reflections on government leaders. The most outrageous, misleading claims and puffs could be launched with impunity from many nations without violating their laws. This country's hard-won and already sadly eroded protection of privacy would be endangered, stripped from the man who takes a girl to the Riviera when he is supposed to be attending a business convention in London as well as from the woman who would not like to see her face or figure used to advertise a deodorant. The standards of our magazines that freely publish photographs of naked black or brown female breasts but rigidly exclude the white bosom will clash with cultures that prohibit pictures of a woman's uncovered face.

If Law can resolve that problem, she may be able to surmount the current dilemma of her own double standard for the print and broadcast media. Government interference with a newspaper or magazine's content is much less than with a radio or television station. The latter are licensed by a Federal commission, but should that subject them to stricter regulation than their press rivals? The government ordered a complete ban on television cigarette advertising on the theory that cigarettes are a health hazard. But does the weed become less of a hazard in a newspaper advertisement? Should the paper continue to corrupt the public? Is the ban an abuse of the licensing power? As these questions become more insistent, Law will have to study her answers.

Copyright protection may need some strengthening too. At present, literary piracy is confined to countries that are not the author's principal market. His resulting losses, while deplorable and in a few cases large, are not crushing. But immunity for a broadcasting source not subject to the international copyright union and capable of reaching a mass public anywhere in the world could destroy any writer's control over his own work and his livelihood along with it. In many nations where illiteracy is high and concepts of literary rights low, this may seem a triviality compared with all the other problems of life—and even a blessing. For example, a third of Africa has no written language of its own, but that will not prevent these countries from having their say about the rules of law for literary property. They may even have sound contributions to make. But it is more likely that if the literate countries do not unite to develop such rules, the marvels of satellite communications may serve in the long run to suppress rather than promote intellectual growth and knowledge. Freedom of expression as we know it could well be lost if the rules that emerge are those of countries where copyright is linked to censorship. Under such law, the pervasive voices and pictures reaching the people by satellite can readily become Big Brother's brainwashing instruments rather than a medium of enlightenment.

Legal questions that can be answered within our own boundaries are cropping up as Comsat, the FCC, and domestic communications titans try to settle on the distribution of satellites in a projected system that would serve the United States exclusively. Law already gives the Commission authority, subject to court review, to set the guidelines for such a device and to issue the licenses without which the satellites may not be operated. Several years of discussion have not as yet led the Commission to a decision. One possibility would be to grant Comsat a monopoly of the domestic satellites, with the FCC regulating rates charged to users. Another proposal, which has a good many supporters in the national administration and the communications world, is for the Commission to support open competition by licensing any well-qualified and well-financed applicant. This assumes that satellite costs can be brought down to compete with ground or wire links for domestic purposes. Then Comsat would enter the domestic field on a par with anyone else who has money and know-how. The American Telephone and Telegraph Company would be able to operate its own, as would the television networks or a major foundation committed to educational programs, or a corporation especially organized for profit. Whichever method the FCC finally chooses, the proponents of the other can be counted upon to contest the decision in the courts. The outcome there will settle some of the new law of space. It will be an important segment because space is limited—even in space. Satellites have to be 5 degrees apart to function properly, so the fight for position will be keen.

Another use of orbiting satellites or manned space platforms can be the maintenance of a more comprehensive inventory of the world's crops, forests, and surface mineral resources than has been possible before. Cameras and electronic sensing devices can send back to a central station within days or weeks data that now takes years to collect and is then obsolete. The practicality has been proved by photographs taken during manned space flights. The National Aeronautics and Space Administration (NASA) is planning to launch the first satellite equipped to study the earth's resources in 1972. When the system is in full operation, the scientists expect better information on crop prospects and needs than is now available, advance warning of volcanic eruptions, and quick, accurate estimates of damage from floods and forest fires. Then will come the questions. Who else should be allowed to establish similar services or seek out other uses for long-distance observations? To what extent would beneficiaries have to submit to regulation?

This is pretty prosaic stuff compared to some of the other prospective uses of space technology. One question for Law will be raised when man's ability to analyze what is below the surface of the earth through an improved sort of X-ray eye is perfected. Science has already received messages from more than 200 miles down, far below the earth's thickest crust. The next step perhaps will be to locate and identify anything as far underground as the technician cares to probe—oil, coal, metals, water. Equally pervasive can be the surveillance of people, with every action, every word, and perhaps even every thought recorded in such detail that the most offensive eavesdropping possible through present electronic devices will seem in retrospect to have been the tools of a golden age of privacy.

Law will move toward regulation of these devices in the

interest of individuals only so far as the public demands control over new forms of exploitation. Entrepreneurs or government officials who spy out underground resources from vantage points in space will hardly disclose their findings to the residents on the surface unless they are obliged by Law to do so.

The sophisticated electronic machines, which may very well return many times over the billions invested in space research, will need some sophisticated legal regulatory machinery if the fruits are to be fairly apportioned. The scramble for wealth revealed from space could easily get out of hand, causing the sort of disputes that accompanied Europeans' discovery of natural riches in America, Asia, and Africa or the exploitation of land and minerals in our own country.

Finally, Law will face the task of control over those highly sensitive devices that will spy on people as well as resources. If Law does not intervene, eavesdroppers on the other side of the world, whether motivated by blackmail or a sincere belief that Big Brother knows best and therefore should know everything, will exercise no restraint. In no aspect of our technological future will it be more important, and in none perhaps more difficult, for Law to manage the machine. The stake here is the personal inviolability of human beings, the preservation of that security of thought and speech without which man might just as well allow himself to be converted into the machine that rules him.

4 | Weather to Order

A century ago, Charles Dudley Warner seemed to have voiced an eternal truth when he said that everybody talks about the weather but nobody does anything about it. Today we are on the verge of repealing this epigram. Changing the weather by human efforts is not only concededly possible, but in some small ways it is being accomplished. Scientists who are engaged in weather research think that their progress in learning the innermost secrets of what makes wind and rain, heat and cold will enable us to modify the weather for our own benefit—they modestly use "modify" rather than "change."

So far, the actual legal issues in weather modifications have centered around a fairly recent technique for extracting rain from clouds that might not otherwise drip at all. Three Americans working for the General Electric Company—Irving Langmuir, a Nobel Prize winner, Vincent Schaefer, and Bernard Vonnegut—did it first in July 1946. Since then, it has been repeated with thousands of clouds all over the world. Acknowledged success has been limited to a few clouds at a time; rainmaking tests over large areas have been inconclusive and controversial, and in at least one elaborate study were reported to have reduced rather than increased rainfall.

The method commonly used is to spray dry ice or silver

iodide into a cloud from an airplane. When the proper proportions are poured out, the chemical crystallizes the cloud's vapor into ice that becomes either rain or snow. Different proportions will dry up the cloud, and this is done to get rid of undesired storms. The exact mechanism of rain, either in nature or helped along by men, is not completely understood. Therefore no one can be quite sure what a given cloud would do if let alone.

Some geographical conditions are more favorable than others, and at times cloud seeding has produced very precise results. Rain has been induced on some fields that needed it while bypassing others nearby where it would have harmed crops. A much more recent technique is to seed two rain clouds as they merge, which is said to increase the yield of rain ten or twenty times.

When cloud seeding gets into the courts, the claims made for it become very modest indeed. The reason it that most of the litigation has been initiated by plaintiffs who asserted either that they were flooded by excessive rain or deprived of moisture by the reverse technique of dissipating clouds to prevent hail storms. On the witness stand, rainmakers have been understandably reluctant to boast that they had done either. None of their cases has been heard in a Federal court.

Auvril Orchard Company Inc. v. Weather Modification Inc. and Apple Weather Inc. is a good example of how state courts approach the problem. The orchard company, whose trees were located near Wenatchee, an apple growing center in the State of Washington, sued for damages caused by heavy flash floods in 1956. Its lawyers argued that the defendants, both cloud-seeding firms hired by neighboring apple growers to break up hail storms, had shifted the precipitation onto Auvril and so caused the floods. On the face of it, this seemed possible, at least to the judge, who granted an injunction that stopped cloud-seeding flights temporarily.

Before the trial of the damage suit came on, he vacated the

injunction and Auvril withdrew its claim. Experts for the cloud-seeders testified that their efforts could not possibly produce that much water. Experts for the orchard company said it was not only possible but plausible. The court found the evidence inconclusive and turned to a similar case decided in Oklahoma three years earlier.

This was a suit brought against one of the most eminent specialists in manipulating clouds, Dr. Irving P. Krick, a Canadian, who was particularly adept at breaking up hail storms. In 1953, his firm had been sued for damages done by a cloudburst. A jury heard the same conflicting testimony that was given later in Wenatchee. The judge charged the jury that the evidence must convince them of two facts before they could award damages. The first was that the cloud seeding did indeed cause a flood that would not have happened in the ordinary course of nature. The second was that the Krick outfit should have known that they were likely to cause the excessive rain and so had been careless. The jury decided that neither of these facts had been proved. The judge in Washington followed a similar line of reasoning in ruling against Auvril. It does not appear that any similar suit elsewhere has succeeded in winning compensation for damages. But Law has stopped some seeding on the grounds that it harmed innocent bystanders.

In 1959, a protest against the seeders was supported by a court in Texas, and on a higher judicial level than hears most weather cases. This dispute originated when farmers in Pecos County hired Southwest Weather Research Inc. to break up hail storms that did a great deal of damage in the lush, irrigated lands around Fort Stockton. The storms were formed in the mountains of Jeff Davis County, an area of ranches, so the company's planes went there to spray them. The spraying was so successful that the clouds disappeared altogether, and the ranchers below complained that they had lost a lot of valuable moisture. For their grass and water holes, it did not matter whether the precipitation was in the form of rain or hail; it was theirs, and they wanted it.

Again the experts differed. Those testifying for the farmers said that cloud seeding sufficient to break up hail storms would increase the rainfall if anything. Those for the ranchers retorted that enough chemical to destroy hail would eliminate or greatly reduce the rain. This time, though, another type of expert appeared, old men who had lived all their lives in the mountains and whose success in ranching and hunting often depended upon their ability to forecast the weather. They were more persuasive than the scientists. Eleven of them swore that they had seen clouds that they knew from long experience would normally produce rain simply vanish just after the planes went over. No damages were asked. The ranchers just asked that the cloud seeding be stopped, and the judge granted an injunction.

That did nothing to protect crops from hail storms, so the farmers took *Southwest Weather Research Inc. v. Rounsaville* to the the Texas Court of Civil Appeals. Here the right of a cloud-seeder to carry on his business was asserted on the basis of the law making the air free to all for purposes of aviation. The three judges in an unsigned opinion pointed out that *U. S. v. Causby* had ruled out improper or unreasonable invasions of the air. (See Chapter 2.) Cloud seeding, to the judges' way of thinking, was not a reasonable extension of the right of transit. They explained:

"We believe that under our system of government, the landowner is entitled to such precipitation as Nature deigns to bestow. We believe that the landowner is entitled, therefore and thereby, to such rainfall as may come from clouds over his own property that Nature, in her caprice, may provide."

However sensible and fair this may seem, it cannot be said to be the law throughout the United States. At the time of the ruling, other courts had considered the problem of who owns the clouds from a somewhat different if not more elevated per-

spective. The issue had arisen in 1950 when New York, endur-
ing one of its worst water shortages in the midst of a severe
drought, employed a cloud-seeder to bring rain over part of the
city's watershed in the Catskill Mountains. This is also a highly
developed resort area, and rain is as bad for resort owners as it
is good for farmers and city reservoirs. Some of the owners
sued to stop New York's attempt to alleviate the drought.

Ben J. Slutsky et al., Co-partners Doing Business under the
Name of Nevele Country Club v. the City of New York was one
of the earlier attempts to have the courts enjoin rainmakers.
The club's lawyers urged, in addition to the harm done to their
client's business, that the cloud-seeder might make so much
rain that streams would overflow and damage property. They
also contended that they and their neighbors owned the clouds
over their land, so that New York City in effect was using their
own property to ruin their business. They informed the court
that this was contrary to both law and morality.

Judge Ferdinand Pecora rejected the argument as a whole
and in detail. The danger of floods and even the threat to business had not been proved to his satisfaction, he said. But he
was satisfied that ten million users of water were in real peril—
he and his family were among them. He relied upon a well-
established legal principle that the admitted rights or interests
of a few people, amply secured in law and custom, must be
sacrificed when they are, as Pecora put it, "opposed to the general welfare and public good." The individuals who suffer
under such circumstances must bear their losses as best they
can. He added:

"This court will not protect a possible private injury at the
expense of a positive public advantage."

The judge went further, declaring that the plaintiffs could
not rely upon the old "sky's the limit" rule of ownership "since
they clearly have no vested property rights in the clouds or the
moisture therein." His decision remains the law in New York as
that of the Civil Court of Appeals remains the law in Texas,

although the two could hardly be more contradictory. States frequently adopt different versions of Law, whether in diametrically opposite legislation or in their judicial interpretations of statute and common law. Far from being deplorable, this is one of the strengths of our Federal system, giving room for many varied experimental and tentative solutions to tough legal problems.

As a result of judicial rulings and popular feelings about rainmakers, nearly half the states have established weather-modification regulations. Some require licenses, given only after a showing of skill and financial responsibility. Some license anyone who applies and pays a fee. Others require reports on each operation, regulate the manufacture and distribution of rainmaking equipment, or authorize no one except public bodies such as municipalities or water districts to try it.

Since 1951, both houses of Congress have talked about a Federal law to regulate weather modification; an act of Congress would preempt the field under either the defense or interstate commerce clauses of the Constitution. Committees have studied the issues involved. Research has been financed. A Federal Advisory Committee on Weather Control was set up, one of whose functions was to watch the various state efforts and figure out which work best. The administration has entrusted the Executive Branch's share of the weather problem to the National Oceanic and Atmospheric Administration in the Commerce Department. In Boulder, Colorado, the National Center for Atmospheric Research, a consortium of seventeen universities, conducts perhaps the most consistently significant studies of the weather that this country supports.

Just forecasting the weather accurately, let alone doing something about it, depends upon what we can learn in space and the upper atmosphere and from the movement of water in the ocean depths. Before any real changes are made, one hopes that Law will catch up with the experimenters to compel them (if they do not do it of their own accord) to feed all their data into a computer and get a report on the result in advance. That would at least avert the danger that men would loose a hurricane while trying to produce a breeze.

All this is preliminary exercise toward the day when the manufacture of weather will be a major industry and a government monopoly. Monopoly will be necessary partly because the job will involve dealing with other countries, and under the Constitution only government is permitted to do that, and partly because weather is too important to entrust to private people. The prospect of letting everyone who can afford the price get the weather he happens to want for pleasure or profit is quite intolerable. We can expect then that one of the chief figures in the President's Cabinet will be a Secretary of the Weather whose department will be entrusted with the delicate and difficult task of deciding the temperature, rainfall, and number of sunny days allotted to each section of the country. He will need great wisdom and incorruptible integrity.

He or his deputies will be key figures in an international body that will be established under Law to divide this "pie in the sky" equitably. Member governments will have to sacrifice a certain amount of national sovereignty, rather more than powerful countries have so far been willing to relinquish. The obvious danger of allowing any to go ahead with major weather modifications regardless of the effect on others may drive the nations to accept international control. None will be willing to allow another to carry out a project that could benefit the sponsor but ruin its neighbors.

Such possibilities are within reach of techniques now known. Some scientists believe they could bring about massive climate changes by sheer man-made power, although for all the awesome energy we have developed by splitting atoms and harnessing rivers, we are still puny as compared to nature. A single one of the hurricanes we call by girls' names every autumn has thousands of times more energy than all the electricity generated in the United States in a year. But before man can match that force, he may be able to interfere with the climatic combinations that give birth to a hurricane and so prevent its formation. By diverting masses of water or air, he might shift cold winds to warm or vice versa, and thereby produce more rain or less, more sunshine or less, a mild or severe temperature over an area of a few hundred square miles.

Law may well be asked to stop weathermaking at that point because going further might well do more damage to one region than any possible benefit to another could justify. At least one proposal for effecting a major revolution in climate has been analyzed, and the results are more frightening than hopeful. Perhaps this is why it is not being attempted although it is theoretically feasible.

Scientists such as Glenn T. Seaborg foresee the day when the necessary force will be at our disposal. As chairman of the Atomic Energy Commission in 1968, Dr. Seaborg predicted the development of nuclear power that would produce an energy source equal to 500 Pacific Oceans full of high-grade petroleum. This would make us a fair match for a hurricane and permit us to pump desalinated sea water into all the deserts of the world. So far as anyone can tell, this would be a clear gain to the world's food and fiber supply and no threat to any other environment.

With less expenditure of energy, we could dam the Bering Strait from Russia to Alaska and pump warm water over it from the Pacific into the Arctic Ocean. Enough water could be shifted to turn the now frozen wastes of Alaska, Canada, and Siberia into temperate lands as fertile as the American Midwest or Western Europe.

That, however, would be only the beginning. The displaced ice and cold water would almost certainly flow west through the Barents Sea and turn south along Europe's west coast. It might push the Gulf Stream off its course. The British Isles, the Scandinavian countries, and probably the whole coast as far as Spain would become as cheerless although not as cold as the pitiless stretches of tundra are now.

A similar land-reclamation project without the Bering Strait dam has been suggested. This would consist of melting the Arctic icepack, using Dr. Seaborg's oceans of nuclear energy. The same parts of Alaska, Canada and Siberia would be turned into garden spots and no cold water would be displaced. But that would not save Western Europe, and this time the United States also would come in for its share of disaster. During the long Arctic summer, the rays of the sun are now reflected back into the atmosphere from the vast white snowfields that cover the icepack. With the snow melted, the sun would warm the water even more. The winds blowing down toward the United States would be so damp that snow would be almost incessant in the mountains for months on end. Slowly, a new ice age would develop over much of the same areas of the Northern Hemisphere that experienced the last one millions of years ago.

Bernt Balchen, the polar explorer, who studied the Arctic climate thoroughly, suggested as recently as 1969 that nature seems to be tending toward this melting of the icepack, aided by an increase in carbon dioxide in the air. Others have replied that the effect may be offset to some extent if men continue their present rate of dust pollution, which prevents much solar energy from reaching the surface of the earth.

The scientific know-how that can bring about such vast changes in the weather will surely be able to develop techniques that will avert catastrophe. The actual means may be as inconceivable today as were nuclear energy and jet airplanes to the scientists of 1937, or electric power and the horseless carriage to their counterparts one hundred years earlier. Whether the protective measures are taken before exploitation gives rise to destructive side effects depends upon Law's ability to keep pace with Science in this field. Already Law can point to precedents that she may apply to the new situations.

One set of legal principles that could prove pertinent derives from the very importance of water, which has been the main object of weather modification up to now. While state laws on the use of streams vary, it is a generally accepted principle that the owner of land upstream cannot divert water at the expense of the owners downstream without paying for it. States enter into legal agreements for the exploitation of rivers. New York did this with its neighbors to get water from the Delaware. Colorado, California and Arizona finally reached a settlement after years of litigation concerning the water of the Colorado River. Seldom are all the parties, either states or private owners along a creek, completely satisfied with their share. But they accept it because the alternative is chaos, with the strongest grabbing everything.

Even more relevant to international control of weather-making are the steps Law has taken to govern the use that nations may make of rivers that flow through more than one country. All around the world, treaties regulate the activities of the signers for mutual protection against each other's greed. In some cases, a multination board or commission oversees the enforcement of the rules. In general, these are intended to guard against the risk that one country bordering on the river will unilaterally change the flow or introduce pollutants that will affect the others. Projects that would produce such effects must be submitted to all signatories. If they object, and the treaties set up procedures to determine whether the objectors are acting in good faith, the plans must be revised to meet the objections or the injured must be paid for any damage. The United States, for instance, has compensated Mexico for the harm done in her territory by our diversion and pollution of Colorado River waters. We use so much water for irrigation within this country that what is left by the time it gets to Mexico is of reduced quality and quantity.

Another example of the international harmony that control of rain and wind will impose upon nations is their present sharing of weather information. Russia and the United States have had a formal agreement on this for years. Whatever is discovered by scientific observation is broadcast to all; no government tries to keep an approaching storm secret. This practice has been carried so far that in 1970, oceanographers, physicists and meteorologists from the U.S.S.R. joined their fellows from eight other countries not in the Soviet orbit in a project sponsored by the United States. The aim was to seek a standard on which all could agree for measuring various phenomena in the sea and air that relate to weather forecasting. The American Environmental Science Services Administration provided the floating laboratory that the expedition used in a cruise on the Gulf of Mexico, the Caribbean Sea, and the Pacific Ocean off the west coast of South America. Recognizing the need for speaking the same scientific language is a modest step toward cooperation in weather control.

One reason for optimism in thinking that Law will be able to achieve this objective is that the potential benefits are so great. Every country could get a generous share and, if Law can arrange adequate safeguards, none need suffer. The rules would have to include prohibition of far-reaching scientific experiments on a massive scale before the scientists have demonstrated that irreparable harm will not follow, and that the experiments are not a deliberate attempt to ruin an enemy. One would expect general acceptance of a treaty outlawing weather as a weapon of war, although in the past, and even in the present, nations have tended to ignore destruction of plant and animal life over large areas by mining and certain military tactics. Territory so devastated has been known to undergo changes of degrees in temperature. The even more drastic possibilities of weather modification, if Law permits exploiters or soldiers or statesmen to undertake it at will, are in themselves a good reason for even the most bellicose of states to abjure the thought.

While irrational, mutually destructive quarrels between

sovereign states are hardly unprecedented, nations do not indulge in them in the presence of a fine, juicy pie that will turn to poison if anyone at the table is left out when it is cut. The benefits of weathermaking are such a pie. Furthermore, Science may set before us other tempting morsels—in outer space, at the bottom of the ocean, by harnessing new sources of energy. The prospect is so mouth-watering that it may well entice the world down the garden path to peace on earth behind the one safe guide to such a Utopia—Law.

5 | The Ocean Depths

Nothing since Europeans stumbled on America has so spectacularly increased exploitable territory as Science's discovery that it can deliver to us the resources of the ocean bottoms. Columbus and his successors brought home great wealth and even greater dreams that still fell short of reality. Today we can hardly predict the booty that we may win under the sea. The few men who have been there have come back with stories as fantastic as those told by the first who reported on the New World. Already both private companies and governments have spent a lot of money on devices to drill for oil or bring up valuable metals from depths that, as recently as 1958, no recognized authority thought could ever be plumbed for practical development. Ten years later, a distinguished oceanographer, Frank Press of the Massachusetts Institute of Technology and NASA's Lunar and Planetary Missions Board wrote:

"The next decade should see many innovations in oceanographic research. The drilling programs will probe the history of the oceans. Much will be learned from a study of the minerals and fossils that will undoubtedly be found from the sedentary rock below. Submarines will penetrate the deepest ocean. Large sections of the ocean will be set aside for agriculture of high-protein food. Oil and minerals will be mined from great depths."

Only a few years ago it seemed reasonable that the law of discovery should apply to land under water as well as to that above. The scientific and technical research required would hardly be undertaken without some prospect of a return to the government or the corporations who shouldered the risk and the expense. "Finders keepers" was surely the simplest and most equitable rule for inspiring the search for oceanic treasure.

In practice, however, the claim to title by discovery has throughout history been superseded by some such slogan as "to the victor belong the spoils." Valuable lands claimed by explorers were retained only by force, whenever the prize was sufficiently glittering to tempt others. The mightiest nations today have little stomach for the centuries of armed strife by which the original European claimants of the rest of the world clung to and shifted ownership in accordance with the fortunes of war. The occasional peaceful exchanges or sales, such as our purchases of Louisiana and Alaska, were exceptions, and even they were usually the by-products of war or the threat of war.

Men have learned enough from this history that by 1968 nations generally accepted the idea that all of the ocean floor beyond the territorial limits of individual countries belongs, as does outer space, to all equally, and to none exclusively. On this basis, the United Nations in March 1968 formed an Ad Hoc Committee on Seabed and Ocean Floor.

At the same time, a detailed program for dealing with the situation by Law was offered in what is believed to be the first treaty ever drafted by a United States senator. The pioneer was Claiborne Pell of Rhode Island, and he was clearly inspired by the agreements already reached concerning space. His draft even referred to the area whose exploration and exploitation it was designed to regulate as "ocean space."

Senator Pell proposed the following as the law of oceans:

No weapons of any kind would be permitted on the floor outside territorial limits. A United Nations Authority would license every human activity under the sea and would have an international navy very like the United States Coast Guard to enforce its regulations. The Authority would specifically establish rules for the disposal of radioactive and other wastes in the ocean. (Such rules, no doubt, would have forbidden the sinking of a United States Army shipload of nerve gas at sea in 1970, an action strongly denounced at the time as a reckless and dangerous reliance on the indestructability of the gas containers.) The Authority would be supplied with electronic and other equipment needed to detect any violations of its orders.

While the major goal of the treaty, establishment of the international authority with enforcement powers, has won little more than lip service from governments, the nations have moved slowly toward a rule of Law on the ocean floor. The United States acted on its own a few months after the nerve-gas dumping, banning by a Defense Department order the disposal of not only gas but obsolete ammunition in this way. The Army had been sinking surplus weapons and explosives at sea for more than a hundred years, but concern for what they may do at the bottom succeeded in reversing a tradition.

In seeking international law on the seabed, the obstacles are greater than in the negotiations over space, no doubt because, for all the glamor of the astronauts, the material potential of the oceans seems closer to realization than that of the moon and the stars. Nations have been unwilling to give up anything that seemed already within their grasp beneath a few miles of water, whereas they are inclined to be generous in sharing the more remote possibilities of space. International dickering dragged along for nearly three years, in formal sessions at both Geneva and New York and in innumerable meetings of experts, before agreement was reached on much of anything.

The course of the talks neatly illustrated the limitations of power. In the very early stages, the United States and Russia agreed on the main provisions of a treaty that would forbid nuclear weapons on the ocean floor outside the 12-mile limit. Russia had wanted all weapons included, as Senator Pell's treaty draft provided, but yielded to the United States position that only nuclear arms should be mentioned. Both countries were content to rely on their own inspection equipment—electronic surveillance from their own surface ships—to detect possible violations. But smaller, weaker countries were not satisfied. Under the leadership of Canada, they fought for and won the right of all nations to obtain United Nations help in checking on compliance. Law that left enforcement to the strongest alone was amended to give the weaker a voice. The United Nations General Assembly on December 7, 1970, recommended the final draft by a vote of 104 to 2. On February 11, 1971, elaborate ceremonies in Washington, London and Moscow accompanied the formal signing by sixty-three nations. However, two of the world's five nuclear powers, France and China, did not sign.

This agreement left virtually all of the other problems of exploring and exploiting the seabed unresolved. The years of talk have failed to establish even the boundaries of the territory under discussion, which would seem an essential starting point. At present, only the relatively shallow waters off the coasts can be penetrated effectively for such productive operations as drilling or mining. And in the last twenty years, most countries with any seacoast at all have widened their claims to the waters they border. In 1951 the 3-mile limit was accepted by forty-five nations. Three claimed 12 miles, and seven, 200 miles. Now, with a number of newly independent states in the picture, nine South and Central American countries insist on 200 miles, and fifty-six assert the 12-mile claim. The 3-mile-limit group has shrunk to thirty. Under United States law, the individual states have authority only within 3 miles and the Federal government beyond that.

One proposal for regulating undersea resources is a depth limit. Another suggestion is that each country restrict its claim of exclusive rights to the continental shelf off its own coast. This is construed as the slope under relatively shallow water before the real ocean depths or abyss. Its width varies from virtually nothing at all off parts of the west coast of South America to many miles. In some places, such as the North Sea, the shelf runs from the shore of one country to that of another. A general agreement as to just how far the continental shelf extended was in effect for a few years, but technology soon outran Law.

In 1958, the representatives of no fewer than eighty-six countries accepted a convention that defined the continental shelf as land under water less than 200 meters or 660 feet deep. The measure won general consent because no one could then exploit the bottom at a greater depth. But almost as soon as this limit was adopted, delegates of various nations argued that by the real meaning of the convention, the continental shelf's boundary was at the depth men could work. This would be meaningless, since drilling and mining at thousands of meters are becoming feasible. Submarines capable of exploring nearly three miles down are projected, and oil drillers are confident that within a decade they will be able to tap a well at any depth.

The 1958 convention did lead to the legal settlement of one dispute. The North Sea, bordered by Great Britain, Germany and the Netherlands, is nowhere more than 200 meters deep. The three countries submitted the problem of jurisdiction to the International Court of Justice, which in 1969 fixed the boundaries.

To overcome the confusion of defining "continental shelf" in terms of water depth, a United States commission has proposed that all nations accept a 50-mile limit, regardless of how far below the surface the bottom may be. Our government has not formally adopted the proposal, nor have other countries.

But at regular United Nations meetings and at special conferences of scientists and lawyers, the question continues to be discussed. Some experts think the delay in reaching conclusions is not a bad thing. They point out that conditions for actually working the ocean floor profitably are so uncertain that it would be reckless to set up rules that may not apply or may even handicap exploitation of the resources when the methods are perfected.

Certainly, Science is not waiting for Law's decisions. A number of large industrial corporations have been doing their own research. Oil companies, as indicated, are well along. Others are working on methods for bringing up rich ores of manganese, copper, nickel, and other valuable metals from 12,000 or 15,000 feet below the surface. Methods of identifying materials deep in the earth, mentioned in Chaper 3, would apply to the seabed too. The government considers all these prospects of such importance that a very high-level council in the Executive Office of the President keeps watch over developments. Since Hubert Humphrey's time, the Vice President has been its chairman. Members are the Secretaries of State, Navy, Commerce, Interior, Transportation, and Health, Education and Welfare, the Chairman of the Atomic Energy Commission, and the Director of the National Science Foundation.

Although United States technicians working for either the government or private organizations are expected to make a large contribution to developing the ocean's resources, this country is virtually committed to earmarking those resources for what President Nixon has called "international community purposes, particularly economic assistance to developing countries." Mr. Nixon explained in May 1970 that our government considers the seabed and all its resources "the common heritage of mankind." It is clear that this heritage could only be put to good use through the medium of such an international governing body as Senator Pell had proposed, if all were to benefit equally, but the President's commitment did not extend that far.

In the same remarks, Mr. Nixon made it quite plain that he would protect the interests of those who invest time, money, and skill in developing the means for oceanic exploitation. Through either the international authority or an agency of their own country, qualified entrepreneurs would be licensed to extract oil or metals, garner food or fiber, or develop whatever resources they can find. They would pay a royalty for this privilege, and the royalties would be the part of the common heritage that all mankind would receive. The theory is not unlike the present system of oil or mining leases in this country. Undoubtedly governments would find it easier to arrange such royalty agreements than to dispose of the proceeds in ways acceptable to all. However, neither developing nor developed countries have evidenced much disposition to quarrel over the division of these spoils. The hunters are waiting to bag their bear before they divide the skin. The skin is what they probably will contest with a bitterness proportional to the value of such legal niceties as hunting licenses, division of the spoils and rights to explore.

Fortunately, nations have been accustomed to the necessity for yielding to Law in dealing with at least some of the riches of the sea. They adopted these working arrangements, it is true, only after wealth had been recklessly dissipated and was in real danger of vanishing entirely. The old rule allowing everyone equal access to the oceans outside territorial waters permitted no control over the greed of any. Typical of the Law devised for such situations are the international sealing and whaling agreements by which the slaughter of these animals is regulated. Countries that can agree on hardly anything else cooperate harmoniously on the commissions that oversee the operation of these treaties.

As instructive in the development of international Law as

the final agreements are the disputes and disasters without which apparently neither nations nor corporations would have consented to legal adjudication of their claims to unrestricted slaughter. Whether the legal lesson learned from seals and whales can be applied to other oceanic treasures is still doubtful.

By the time the United States bought Alaska from Russia in 1867, virtually all the world's seals were extinct, except those whose rookeries were on the Pribiloff Islands in the Bering Strait. Our government began serious efforts at regulation in 1872, but neither the company to which it leased exclusive sealing rights nor poachers from other countries paid any attention. A bitter dispute with Great Britain grew out of the United States claim to a monopoly. The quarrel went before an international arbitration tribunal in Paris in 1893. The verdict was that the United States had no valid claim to seals in the open sea, so killing there was open to anyone, and the United States must pay damages for interfering with others. The resulting slaughter reduced the herd enormously, and efforts to protect the rookeries were steadily evaded by the company that had the exclusive lease, aided by the Commissioner of Fisheries and his underlings.

Conservationists disclosed that the company was partly owned by Senator Stephen B. Elkins of West Virginia, one of the great land grabbers of the Southwest and a major boodler of the East, and the Commissioner was his man. The revelations had no effect upon enforcement of the rules, although a Congressional investigation exposed the violations and named officials who condoned them. By 1910, only about 130,000 fur-bearing seals were left alive on the Pribiloff Islands. With extinction of the species imminent, the exploiters turned their attention to more profitable loot. Then the four sealing nations— the United States, Great Britain, Japan and Russia—finally agreed to a treaty that outlawed the hunting of seals until the herd was built up, and provided for future regulations to limit the catch. The treaty was signed in 1911 and is rightly considered one of the triumphs of international law. But it took a lot of illegality to produce the state of public opinion that made it possible.

The whaling agreement owed more to advancing technology than to boodlers but reached fruition only after whales were also threatened with extinction. The animals won a reprieve when gas, kerosene and electricity for lighting replaced whale oil to a great extent, and fashion discarded whalebone. But technology came to the whaler's rescue. A Norwegian invented a harpoon with an explosive head, which killed a whale instantly so that none got away. The modern factory ship enables the crew to cut up and bring home the whole beast for various uses, including meat. The ardent defense of seals had only a faint counterpart when it came to protecting whales, but the declining whale population at length led to a treaty in 1946. The international whaling commission sets the now relatively short season for the kill and the size of whales that are fair game.

An international authority to regulate and police human exploitation of the ocean floor may well be modeled on these commissions. It would need rather more authority than they possess, and, of course, its scope would have to be far wider. One of the issues, perhaps the first, that faces Law in this field is how to regulate scientific experiments and their application so as to prevent the sort of contamination in the ocean that has ruined considerable parts of the land. Controls to assure the safety of the deep are obviously needed now to minimize the danger of radiation from nuclear power used under water or reckless dumping of oil waste and other noxious refuse. Reliance upon national law to preserve international interests has proved ineffective. A Sea Law Conference is scheduled for 1973, and some new treaty provisions might emerge from it. Perhaps enough demand has been engendered that the delegates will at least develop a legal rule to last a few years on where international waters begin—whether in miles out from the coast or in meters of depth. By then, nations may be sufficiently aware of the dangers inherent in uncontrolled seabed exploitation to consider seriously the establishment of such an international authority as Senator Pell proposed.

Part Two

LAW AND THE
SPACESHIP EARTH

6 | In Search of Energy

Electricity may not make the world spin, but it keeps the American way of life going so fast that we double the amount we consume every ten years. As technology calls for more and more energy, we may even get to the point where each of us will use as much as a Norwegian—Norway's per capita consumption is about double ours. But we have a few hurdles to surmount first. One is to find new sources. Already a power failure in any part of the country disrupts our routine more than the loss of almost all other amenities put together. Electricity does so much of our hard, dirty work that it occupies in our Pantheon the place ancient Egyptians accorded the Nile flood—the niche of a perennial, inexhaustible, omnipotent benefactor. Steam and the internal combustion engine did their share, but electricity is now more important than both combined, and many people would like to see it replace both.

Falling water was the first great source of this energy, then oil, gas and coal, and more recently atomic fission. Each has presented us with its own subsidiary problems. Rivers with falls or rapids of sufficient force are too few to meet more than a fraction of the demand. Gas is scarce. Coal and oil pollute the air unless very expensively controlled, and at the rate we use power it may soon be insufficient anyway. Modern generating plants are so big that a new one in the Nevada desert, built to produce a million and a half kilowatt hours and equipped to allow only 3 percent of its fly ash to escape—pretty clean by the best modern standards—will still emit about 24 tons of dust a day. Atomic or nuclear generators present some not completely understood dangers of radiation and one very clear problem of excessive heat.

Law stepped in early to fix rates for electricity after granting monopolies for its distribution, and to establish safety standards. Now she is called upon to hold a balance between Science's ability to release limitless oceans of nuclear energy and the risks involved in the process. Law's expertise for this task has been developed in the solutions she gave to problems posed by earlier machines invented to replace muscle.

The impact of Science upon Law in this field can be traced to the times of Coke and Bacon when lawyers began to change their trial system from a test of deductive reasoning to an inquiry into facts revealed by evidence. Instead of concluding that God would not allow an innocent man's hand to burn if it were thrust into a fire when he was accused of theft, Law asked for proof that the fellow had stolen. The same method of inquiry led Copernicus to his heretical discovery that the sun, not the earth, is the center of our universe. The new idea of jurisprudence liberated scientists. It freed them from being condemned, like Galileo, when their newly stated truths contradicted revealed religion or traditional beliefs. It was no mere coincidence that the first attempt to systematize Law by collecting significant cases and arguing from past experience, begun by Sir Matthew Hale about 1673, followed by less than a decade the foundation of the first modern scientific body, the Royal Society.

However much Law owed to the method of Science—and it can be argued that lawyers like Bacon gave more than they received—the role of the machine did not seriously challenge legal principles until a little more than a century ago.

Until well past the middle of the 19th century, Law held generally that on your own property you could build anything you liked, set up any machinery, or try out any industrial process. If someone got hurt or the property of others was damaged, you would have to pay only if the victim could prove you were negligent. If you did not know that your machine was dangerous or a substance you made might explode, Law would not hold you liable for the results of an accident. The notion that you might be harming the land around you or the air above or the streams whose water you used occurred to neither Science nor Law. If they noticed such injury to man or nature, it was accepted as the inevitable cost of "progress."

As society and technology both became more intricate, Law began to have second thoughts. These crystalized in England in a famous case known as *Rylands v. Fletcher,* decided in 1868 by the highest appeals tribunal, the House of Lords. When acting as Britain's supreme court, this body delegates the function to the "law lords," the top appeals judges of the land. Their decision in this case is best known to laymen because dozens of novelists have quoted or cited it when a fictional wild beast or poisonous snake gets loose from a circus or laboratory to terrorize a city. The plot gains a spicy twist when someone recalls that, according to *Rylands v. Fletcher,* anyone who "brings on his land and collects or keeps there anything likely to do mischief if it escapes" incurs absolute liability for the resulting damage. However, their lordships were not talking about a ferocious lion or deadly cobra. They referred to energy for driving machines.

Fletcher was a miller, and the wheels of his mill were turned directly by water. He needed a reservoir to ensure a steady flow, so he built one on his own land. When he filled it, enough water leaked out through an abandoned shaft to flood the workings of Rylands's adjacent mine. The mineowner, although he conceded that Fletcher could not be expected to know about the abandoned shaft and had not been in the least negligent in building his reservoir, claimed compensation for the damage to his property. The millowner's position was that since he had been neither careless nor malicious, the court should consider the damage as if it had been done by excessive rain or a flooding river. Counsel for Rylands retorted that rain and floods were acts of God, but the reservoir was the work of man. The judges had to decide whether this made any difference.

The final opinion was that it did. The rain or flood came about during what Lord Cairns, who wrote for the Lords, called a natural use of the land. In such a case, Rylands's neighbors would have nothing to do with the water; they did not bring it in. But a reservoir was not the natural use of the land. When Fletcher brought in and collected all that water, he must have known it would do great damage if it escaped. So he was responsible and must pay.

Since we inherited Law from England, such decisions have great effect in the United States. *Rylands v. Fletcher* is widely accepted in American courts, but not in all. The highest tribunals of at least a dozen states have repudiated it. Two cases in which it was pleaded and then decided in exactly contrary fashion illustrate the arguments for and against the principle it embodies. One is *Berry v. Shell Petroleum Company,* decided in Kansas in 1934. The other is a 1936 Texas lawsuit, *Turner v. Big Lake Oil Company.* In both, the cause of action was that salt water from the defendants' drilling operations leaked into the plaintiffs' water supplies—on Berry's farm and Turner's ranch. Both pointed out that salt water ruined their businesses. Both companies pleaded that salt water is an inevitable by-product of oil drilling, which is so important to the general welfare that Law should ignore the incidental suffering of a few; otherwise the cost of gasoline would rise. Lawyers in both trials cited *Rylands v. Fletcher* and admitted no negligence by the drillers was alleged. Both high courts expressed their sympathy with the oil companies. But after kind words for Shell, the Kansas judges awarded damages to the farmer, saying:

"It is . . . no new principle we are announcing. It is as old as the industry of man. We consider that the water supply of the people is of greater importance than the operation of a business at a reduced cost."

The Texas judges held that the rancher would have to prove negligence to collect damages. They rejected the principle of *Rylands* by name on the ground that "in Texas we have conditions very different from those which obtain in England." Although they did not say so, one of the obvious differences was that oil extraction was relatively much more important to their economy than in that of either the United Kingdom or Kansas.

These contradictory decisions are a good example of Law's response to the demands or desires of the public. In the long run, even the Supreme Court, as Mr. Dooley noted more than fifty years ago, follows the election returns. The people get the Law of energy, as they get all other Law, that they insist upon. As the needs for power develop, from Fletcher's reservoir to gigantic structures producing millions of kilowatt hours of electricity, the courts as well as the legislatures have been responsive to public pressure. For the most part, this has been simply for more and cheaper power. Only in the last few years has Law been asked to consider the price in health, scenery or wildlife.

The Consolidated Edison Company of New York is acutely aware of the questions these new factors raise, and has been frustrated by the answers Law gives. The company is responsible for meeting New York City's enormous demands for electricity. It has been quite unable to execute its ideas of how to do it in the face of popular and legal objections. As a result, Con Edison can no longer satisfy the city's growing appetite for air conditioning during especially hot spells and for heat and power during protracted cold snaps. Its particular crisis, not unlike those of many other utilities, has been more than ten years in the making. Part of a chapter in Law has been written in the process.

The story begins on December 10, 1960, when Con Edison applied to the Atomic Energy Commission for a license to build the first nuclear power plant ever proposed inside a big city. At the time, AEC regulations forbade reactors of the size planned within seventeen miles of large centers of population. This one was to be located in the borough of Queens about a mile and a half from Times Square. Five million New Yorkers lived within a radius of five miles. The prospect of an atomic neighbor scared a large percentage of them.

Con Edison tried to soothe these fears. It pointed out that its big plant would not be finished until 1970. Then it would be housed within walls of concrete and steel seven and a half feet thick. All emissions of smoke or radiation would emerge from a chimney 500 feet tall to be dissipated harmlessly in the air. Any explosion like that of an atomic bomb would be impossible because the fuel would not be arranged in so destructive a pattern. Experts offered their assurances that the plant would be as safe as anything in town, and safer than much. Other experts of equal standing were not so sure. The opinions were summed up in nontechnical terms by David Lilienthal, who had been first chairman of the AEC, and Dr. Seaborg, his successor. The first said he would not live in the same borough with a million-kilowatt reactor. The second said he would be willing to live next door.

Law that might apply was canvassed extensively but not actually tested. Groups of citizens formed to sue to prevent the company from going ahead with its plans even if the AEC granted a license. Queens members of the City Council drafted an ordinance to forbid big reactors inside the city limits but permitting the small ones used by university and industrial researchers. Legal authorities argued as to whether such a law could stand against a license given by an agency created by

Congress for the purpose. The controversy went on for three years. It ended early in 1964 when Con Edison withdrew its application and announced that it would get the extra energy it needed over long transmission lines from Canada. Satisfying the growing demand with new conventionally fueled plants within the city was foiled by the air pollution from low-grade coal, which is plentiful, and the scarcity of natural gas, which is clean.

With these two eliminated and long-line transmission increasingly costly, the scene of battle shifted. Technicians hit upon a plan for using power available during hours of little demand to create energy for the peak periods of the day and year. Some thirty miles up the Hudson River from the city is one of the most picturesque spots along the Palisades, Storm King Mountain. Con Edison proposed to build here a huge reservoir into which it would pump water from the river with power transmitted from city generators when demand was slack. That water pouring down a gigantic trough to be carved in the face of the Palisades would generate two kilowatts for every three that it took to lift the water to the top.

Protests promptly came from two sources. Citizens who lived along the Hudson and loved the scenery called the plan a desecration of nature. Villages and counties through which the company proposed to run its transmission lines on high towers complained that property values would be lowered and tax receipts reduced. The first group, organized as the Scenic Hudson Preservation Conference, led the struggle in the courts, and the aesthetic issue dominated the arguments.

Law provides that projects of this kind must be licensed by the Federal Power Commission. Con Edison had no trouble getting a permit. The act of Congress creating the Commission emphasized its duty to approve applications that foster the development of power. But also mentioned as desirable were "other beneficial public uses, including recreational purposes." Scenic Hudson contended that the Commission had not sufficiently considered the effect of the Storm King project on recreation, the environment generally, and the beauty of the Palisades particularly. At this time, Law was a little vague as to who is entitled to raise these considerations.

When Scenic Hudson filed its suit to block the Storm King license, naming the Commission as well as Con Edison as defendants, the right of private citizens to question a government agency in the courts was generally limited to those who had some material interest in the matter. This long-standing rule was designed to keep the wheels of justice from being clogged by fanatics and troublemakers with no real stake in the issue, individuals fighting a tax they were not called upon to pay or a highway that did not touch their land. The theory was that agencies such as the FPC, created for the purpose, safeguard the public's interest against corporations. It was supposed that if any member of the public could drag the agency into court whenever he wished, the result would be chaos. Law said in effect to the disgruntled citizen, "Don't cry until you're hurt." Members of Scenic Hudson obviously had not yet been hurt. If the completed project injured them in person or property, they should then seek damages—from Con Edison, not the government. Statutes that set up the agencies did allow what they always called "aggrieved persons" the privilege of suing for their rights. But this had been interpreted as applying only after the grievance was demonstrable by admissible legal evidence.

Law had somewhat modified this position before 1965, partly because regulatory agencies almost invariably come to partake of the attitudes and beliefs of the people they are supposed to regulate. Most of an agency's work is concerned with improving the standards and performance of an industry. Officials who sympathize with anything that makes the industry stronger easily disregard incidental damage to the public. But when Law did change this rule about who could sue, political liberals who now used the decision against Con Edison's project had denounced it because it was handed down in favor of business.

The earlier case had arisen during World War II when the Department of the Interior, acting under authority granted by Congress, ordered the price of coal raised as of October 1, 1942. Associated Industries of New York state, a trade association of manufacturers, sued to prevent the order from going into effect. Government counsel tried to have the case thrown out of court on the ground that the association lacked standing. Concededly the order was going to cost each user of coal a little money, but that did not make them "aggrieved" because the order benefited all consumers by assuring an adequate coal supply. The argument was heard by a three-man U.S. Court of Appeals, to which some cases against Federal agencies may be taken in the first instance. Judge Jerome Frank, a pillar of Franklin D. Roosevelt's New Deal in its early days, wrote the opinion, and surprised some liberals by agreeing with the manufacturers.

The mere fact that the order would raise the plaintiffs' cost of doing business did not confer standing upon them, he wrote. On this point, he thought the definition of "aggrieved" was what it always had been. But he and his two colleagues said that the association also was in court "in order to vindicate the public interest." Judge Frank pointed out that the Attorney General could demand a court review of an agency's actions to force officials to safeguard the public, and added:

"Such persons [the New York manufacturers], so authorized, are, so to speak, private Attorneys General."

The fact that "to vindicate the public interest" they were also seeking their private interest was irrelevant, the judge added, and cited two Supreme Court decisions as support. Both involved the efforts of radio stations to set aside orders of the Federal Communications Commission that increased plaintiffs' competition. The Commission said they had no standing, but the Supreme Court had disagreed.

"No person is to have anything in the nature of a property right as a result of the granting of a license," the opinion in *FCC v. Sanders Radio* stated in rejecting the station's plea that the Commission's decision hurt financially. "Plainly it is not the purpose of the Act to protect a licensee against competition but to protect the public."

That last phrase, not the possible loss of money, gave Sanders a right to his day in court. They must not argue for their own interest but to explain, if they could, how the order would prevent the broadcasters involved from serving their listeners as effectively as possible.

When the same Court of Appeals for the Second Circuit decided the fate of the Storm King project 23 years later, it quoted with approval Judge Frank's remark about "private Attorneys General." The new opinion's author, Judge Paul R. Hays, brushed aside the argument that Scenic Hudson had to have some economic interest, as the manufacturers had had in 1942, commenting that "the Supreme Court has not made economic injury a prerequisite where the plaintiffs have shown a direct personal interest." The defendants had also objected that to give Scenic Hudson standing would open up "horrendous possibilities" of hundreds, even thousands, of frivolous lawsuits.

"Our experience with public actions confirms the view that the expense and vexation of legal proceedings is not lightly undertaken," Judge Hays wrote.

On the strength of the aesthetic, recreational, and environmental issues, the project was halted.

This ruling seemed to be the law of the land for five years. Then in 1970, Con Edison tried again for a Storm King reservoir and the FPC approved, while on the other side of the country another Court of Appeals (for the Ninth Circuit) delivered itself of an opinion that directly contradicted *Scenic Hudson*. This one threw out a suit brought by the Sierra Club, an institution of even greater prestige and scope than the New York group, to block a Federally licensed Walt Disney resort in a wilderness area of the Sierra Nevada Mountains. The Ninth Circuit held that the club had no standing, and until the Supreme Court resolves this issue, no one can tell which of these two august tribunals has spoken for Law.

In the end, Con Edison may have to settle for energy produced at a distance. That will depend not only on Science's now timid search for other sources of energy—from the sun or the tides, earth's internal heat or a technique called magneto-hydrodynamics, or from still less known sources—but on Law's gropings toward balance of risk versus benefit in nuclear energy. The AEC has almost monopolized the energy-research dollar because the whole field of atomic fission has been pretty much a by-product of the defense buildup, to which the other sources of energy would contribute little. So far, Law has not been able to safeguard the people and their environment without placing barriers in the way of a rapid growth of nuclear power plants. These now supply a little more than ten percent of the electricity we use; it has been estimated that within twenty years they will have to supply more than half, and that half will be double all the electricity used today. But people no more want a power plant next door than they do a drug clinic or a firehouse or a garbage-disposal station. Yet the same people want a lot of electricity, as they want addicts cured, fires put out, and garbage removed. So they pass the dilemma along to Law.

One solution might be steps to force more rapid development of ways to make electricity that are as clean as electricity itself. But most research money in the field has been invested in atomic energy, and Science is being pressed to find out the full effects of nuclear power operations. The one thing certain now is that the men who have had most to do with nuclear development do not agree on a prognosis. They admit to large areas of ignorance about the danger of serious accidents, the long-range peril from radiation, and the dispersion of the heat produced during power generation.

The last has already led to a considerable amount of legislation forcing technology to build plants that cool the water before returning it to the lake or stream from which it came. The states of Oregon and Washington have fixed 68° as the maximum to which the Columbia River can be heated. Vermont forbids any heating of the Connecticut River within its boundaries in summer, with the result that power companies spent $6,000,000 on cooling towers. A suit in Chicago against the Commonwealth Edison Company's nuclear plant going up north of the city on Lake Michigan is expected to lead to some decisions as to how much heat the lake can stand. Preliminary studies suggest that one or two big nuclear plants might be harmless but more could raise the temperature of the water several degrees. This issue becomes one for the control of water pollution generally rather than of power production.

Popular fears of nuclear plants as potential atomic bombs have led to several legal tests. The Supreme Court had its first tussle with the problem in the spring of 1961. The justices were called upon to interpret several safety provisions that Congress had written into the Atomic Energy Act of 1954: (1) Before the AEC gives a permit to build an atomic plant, it must hold feasibility hearings at which safety is of first importance. (2) After the plant is built, the Commission must hold further hearings to satisfy itself that "adequate protection to the health and safety of the public" is assured before actual operation is licensed. (3) Because the amount of damage from an accident in one of these plants can approach the astronomical, the AEC must have half a billion dollars to meet the claims of victims over and above their own insurance.

The Power Reactor Development Company applied for a permit under this Act in January, 1956. It proposed to build a "breeder reactor" on Lake Erie about half-way between Detroit and Toledo to generate electricity for this area of about two million people. Named for Enrico Fermi, one of the fathers of the atomic bomb, the plant was to incorporate the latest safety devices. The building itself would be capable of containing an explosion equivalent to that of 10,000 tons of TNT or a small atom bomb. The engineers who designed it said this was a greater force than the plant could possibly produce no matter what happened. Because, by one of the miracles of nuclear science, the reactor produced twelve units of fissionable materials for every ten it consumed, controls were included to slow it up when desired and to shut it down automatically if the breeding process became too lively.

While the application was pending, the AEC reported that it was not sure how much dangerous radiation could escape during actual operations. The reactor might release "significant quantities of fission products to the atmosphere." Nevertheless, the AEC in August granted a construction permit, and a five-year legal battle was on. Three labor unions—electrical workers, automobile workers, and papermakers—asked the AEC to revoke the permit until safe operation of the plant could be assured.

The company, during several months of hearings, said that building the plant presented no hazards of radiation, and therefore the Commission did not need to apply the same stringent safety standards that would be required for a license to operate. At that time, the risks could be more reasonably assessed than was possible from plans. The unions retorted that the act of Congress made no such distinction. They added that the plant would cost so much—the estimate was $80,000,000—that pressure to license it would be so great as to lift the burden of proving safety from the company and oblige its critics to prove the plant unsafe. The AEC accepted the company's argument and confirmed the permit, whereupon the unions took the case to the Court of Appeals.

Here both sides mentioned *Rylands v. Fletcher*. The unions pointed out that the company was surely bringing in something "likely to do mischief if it escapes." The company replied that the act of Congress provided for that, if indeed it should happen, through the half billion of extra insurance. The union argument prevailed, and in mid-1969 the Court, by a two to one vote, ordered the permit canceled. This time the company appealed, and the Supreme Court heard the arguments all over again.

As so often happens, all nine justices agreed that the law was perfectly clear and that safety was plainly the primary factor to be considered. But they did not agree as to what the law meant or what considerations of safety dictated. Both opinions said that in the debate over the bill, senators clearly revealed the intent of Congress, but justices deduced quite opposite meanings from the same words.

For the majority of seven, Justice William J. Brennan, Jr., wrote that the AEC was empowered to determine the safety standards needed at each step of construction and operation. He pointed out that the Act specifically permitted and even encouraged the Commission to take a new look before licensing an actual start, a fact well understood by the company. He explained optimistically that knowledge about nuclear reactors was developing so fast that "problems which seem insuperable now may be solved tomorrow, perhaps in the very act of construction itself."

Justice William Douglas, speaking for a minority of two, could see nothing in the act of Congress that permitted the AEC to set different safety standards for construction and operation. He thought that safety must be established "positively" at the outset. He called the stand of the Commission and his seven brethren "with all deference, a lighthearted approach to the most awesome, the most deadly, the most dangerous process that man has ever conceived." He also quoted the Joint Congressional Committee, which supervises the work of the AEC, as noting that the Act "requires the issuance of a license if the construction is carried out in accordance with the terms of the construction permit." Justice Brennan declined to take the committee's remarks seriously, saying:

"The best we can say about this statement, with all deference, is that it must have been inadvertent."

Justice Douglas repeated a passage from the Senate debate that had been noted by the Court of Appeals majority. The text, he said, "makes clear that the time when the issue of 'safety' must be resolved is before the Commission issues a construction permit." Justice Brennan had read the same passage and concluded that it obviously referred only to irrelevant procedural matters. (It might be supposed that the justices would ask the senators what they meant, but judges usually are convinced that they can tell what a legislator's words were intended to convey better than the man himself, especially after a lapse of six or seven years. Besides, court hearings are protracted enough. If the highest national tribunal did not make its own interpretations of what is in the record, the talk as to who meant what would be endless.)

This 1961 decision established the AEC as final authority on safety in the nuclear field but not necessarily for all time. Since the Commission promotes the use of nuclear energy and finances most research in the field, questions have been raised as to its impartiality in ruling on the quality of its own work. Like other agencies, it has tended to absorb the thinking of the people it regulates. Some leading atomic scientists have criticized its safety standards as too low, and legal tests of its powers have been renewed.

In the case of the Enrico Fermi plant, the Commission proved less than omniscient. The supposedly infallible automatic controls failed to detect an unforeseen, highly technical complication that caused a dangerous speeding up of the reactor soon after it began operations. Before a major accident occurred—the University of Michigan Engineering Research Institute estimated the death toll might have reached 67,000—alert engineers spotted the danger signals. The plant was closed for four years.

Considering the vast amount of nuclear construction for

both military and civilian purposes, fatalities have been relatively few. *The New York Times* on July 16, 1970, quoted unnamed critics as putting the deaths in atomic energy plants at 200. In 1961, two soldiers and a sailor were killed in an explosion inside the AEC testing station on the Lost River in Idaho. The radiation was so intense that it took nearly three weeks to decontaminate the bodies sufficiently for burial. Other deaths of workers have been attributed to the accumulated effects of radiation in the plants.

Recently the AEC has been accused of fixing radiation limits dangerously high to favor its own projects, although it has lowered them twice since 1947. It has set 170 milirads (or thousandths of a "rad") as the maximum that a person can absorb safely in a year. A "rad" is short for "Radiation Absorbed Dose," so the reportedly safe amount annually is about one-sixth of a dose. Two of the Commission's own scientists have reported that if everyone got what the AEC calls a safe dose, deaths from cancer and leukemia would increase by at least 16,000 a year, maybe 24,000. Although the AEC scoffs, Law has been invoked.

Minnesota made a frontal legal attack by adopting a statute limiting any nuclear plant to emission of 17 milirads, one-tenth the permitted AEC dose. The Northern States Electric Company, licensed by the Commission to operate a facility in Minnesota, sued to have the law set aside. The case went to a Federal rather than a state court because the Federal government has preempted the field. Wisconsin, Illinois, Michigan, Maryland, Pennsylvania and Vermont intervened on the side on Minnesota. They all contend that although the people are not allowed to permit looser safety standards than those of the AEC, they may require stricter ones. As this is written, the courts have not yet ruled.

An important influence on the decision, no doubt, will be just how many cases of cancer, leukemia, and birth defects 170 milirads do cause. Linus Pauling, a Nobel Prize winner in nuclear physics, pointed out in the September 1970 issue of the *Bulletin of Atomic Scientists* that no one now knows how much of the damage is done by the natural background of high energy radiation that has always been present and how much by man's own activities. He estimated that out of 80,000 babies born with mental or physical defects caused by mutations of the genes, 8,000 can be attributed to this uncontrollable background radiation. In our present state of ignorance, we cannot be sure about the rest. Before Law can give intelligent guidelines on this issue, it will need more help from Science.

It might be supposed that citizen groups would be suing to block the building of nuclear plants for fear of accidents or excessive radiation. But they have been denied standing as "private Attorneys General" in this field. In *Pauling et al v. McElroy et al,* 39 citizens sued the Department of Defense and the AEC to stop nuclear explosions that might cause radiation. Turned down in Federal District Court, they went on to the Court of Appeals. The three judges told them they had no standing because "they do not allege a specific threatened injury to themselves apart from others." The Supreme Court affirmed this decision in 1960 by refusing to entertain a further appeal.

Law has drawn a line against what she considers frivolous suits that waste a court's time, but she constantly shifts that line to meet new situations and changing ideas. Nowadays, citizens may have standing if they can produce a valid threat to scenery or recreation or perhaps the environment, although Law held these irrelevant a few years ago. A group of Cornell professors in 1970 forced the abandonment of plans for a nuclear plant near them because they were preparing a suit based on overheating Lake Cayuga. Five nuclear projects in other parts of the country were similarly prevented, and one authority on environmental law has written that such a threat is an effective legal ploy because a utility will usually go away and try in another location rather than undertake a long, expensive trial.

Nor is the citizen helpless if he can prove an injury, even one resulting from the Army's purportedly essential activities. That was decided as far back as 1953 when bomb tests above ground were still conducted. On St. Patrick's Day that year, a relatively small bomb, equivalent to only 15,000 tons of TNT, was exploded in the Nevada desert at Yucca Flats, a project called Operation Upshot-Knothole. The mushroom cloud, seen by millions on television, rose 40,000 feet into the air and scattered what is now recognized as a dangerously large amount of radioactive dust, so much and so widely that it could be measured in the air over Ohio two days later. At the time, AEC scientists assured the country that this radiation was harmless, but even then their opinion was questioned, and in a court too.

When Upshot-Knothole was loosed, herds of sheep were only about fifty miles away in Utah. During the next few weeks, such an unusually large number of them died that their owners called on the Army to pay for the loss. The Army refused, and several sheepmen sued. The case of one named Bulloch was chosen as a test of the government's liability. Because it was a test, United States District Judge A. Sherman Christenson allowed both sides the widest possible latitude in presenting their facts and expert opinions. From the government's point of view, the most important issue was that it be exempt from payment even if radiation from Upshot-Knothole did the damage. The explosion was "a discretionary function of government" in accordance with national policy, so that if a citizen was hurt it was just too bad. Judge Christenson was impressed by the skill and diligence with which this argument was presented, but he was not convinced. He said it would in effect deny "fundamental human rights for the protection of which our governmental policy is designed." He also pointed out that the Army had not lived up to its legal obligation to warn Bulloch and the others to get their sheep out of the danger zone, just as "men at work" signs alert motorists and pedestrians when streets are torn up.

Unfortunately for the sheepmen, the evidence did not prove that radiation killed the sheep. The bulk of the expert testimony indicated that they died of a combination of infections, too little food, and an unusually severe cold snap. *Bulloch v. U.S.*, however, established that in law the government is obliged to warn people of their danger when atomic energy is released and perhaps pay for damages anyway. While tests in the atmosphere are now forbidden, the AEC scheduled 23 of them underground during 1970, and controversy over some of the earlier ones has been pushing Law toward new thoughts on rules to control this genie before he gets all the way out of his bottle.

Four court suits to block a 1969 AEC experiment to release natural gas by an underground explosion were lost. But within a year after the blast was let loose, 355 claims for damages done above ground had been filed, and the AEC had settled more than $90,000 worth of them before trial. Also in 1969 and also in Colorado, the Rocky Flats plant of the Dow Chemical Company, which makes plutonium triggers for hydrogen bombs under an AEC contract, suffered a fire that consumed $45,000,000 in property inside the plant itself. The argument over how far the released plutonium had spread and the danger it posed was still going on a year and a half later. By that time, the last of 1970's underground tests, on December 18, in the already heavily contaminated Nevada desert, broke through the surface and spread radioactive dust across part of Utah. At least fourteen other underground tests have each leaked into the air an amount of radioactivity estimated as equal to that of the Hiroshima bomb.

Besides warning against radiation from normal nuclear energy operation and the danger of accidents, some critics of AEC complain about the disposal of wastes from these plants. The wastes contain enormous concentrations of radioactive substances that will remain deadly for about 500,000 years unless Science finds some as yet unsuspected way of defusing them. The rate of accumulation of such wastes had reached 100,000 gallons a year, most of it stored in remote underground tanks. On December 15, 1970, *Look* magazine quoted a National Academy of Sciences committee as warning AEC that none of the sites "is geologically suited" to the safe disposal of these wastes. The chief danger is that if they leak—and the stuff is very active—they will contaminate drinking water that trickles through bedrock and soil over vast areas.

Abandoned salt mines offer a possible solution, for salt is a good shield against radiation and a stable substance. When the AEC found such a mine under the town of Lyons, Kansas, early in 1971 and asked Congress for $3,500,000 to buy it, conservationists were quick to demand that the Commission take its deadly wastes elsewhere. The outcry was as bitter as if the suggestion were for a power plant or a low-cost housing project. But in this instance, the objections did not come from the people of Lyons. According to a report by a *New York Times* correspondent, 99 out of 100 of them were content to live above the storage, for they believed government experts who assured them the wastes, as the AEC would handle them, could never leak or break out.

In the light of all these nuclear dangers, the pressure to alleviate them through Law is bound to increase. At present, the reassurances of AEC spokesmen and the alarms sounded by the Commission's critics are based as much on speculation as on knowledge. Therefore, Law finds itself in the position it occupied when it had to determine questions of life or death through ordeal by fire or water. Before Law can step in with its proper balancing act of risks versus benefits, Science will have to provide more precise evidence than it has so far as to what nuclear energy will not only give but what it will cost.

7 | The Legality of Dirt

The human race runs a dirty ship, and most of the dirt today is produced by machines and processes unknown a century or two ago. In those days, it is true, men's persons, homes, and habits were filthier than they are now. The cabins where people lived on the good ship Earth were a mess, but the rest of the ship was clean. The inhabitants just did not know how to foul up earth as Science has since enabled them to do. And for a long time the technologists and engineers did not realize what they were doing. Everyone took it for granted that rivers and lakes would carry off any amount of waste we dumped into them, that wind would blow away whatever noxious gases and dust we released into the air, that the soil would absorb and somehow purify all the litter we scattered over it.

Eventually, scientists, with a few assists from concerned laymen, began to learn about the unwanted and undesired by-products of scientific progress, and Law is now being called upon to help the technicians clean up. As long as the only objection to dirt was on aesthetic grounds, the objectors made little progress, although England adopted a smoke abatement law as early as 1273, and a violator in 1307 is said to have been executed. But coal increasingly replaced wood and charcoal until nearly five hundred years later Shelley wrote: "Hell is a city much like London—a populous and smoky city."

Protests then and for a long time afterward were confined largely to poets and other finicky types. Only a few years ago, fears that the affluent society was poisoning itself with its own wastes were dismissed as the vaporings of crackpots and alarmists. Now they have become a major issue in politics. At all levels of government, agencies are being set up to protect the environment from Science or with the help of Science.

The legal basis for such protection seems at first glance to be solid. Any industrial process, any public or private waste disposal, any individual machine that emits harmful or unsightly substances is a nuisance, and a large respectable body of Law deals with the elimination of nuisances. Furthermore, anyone—individual, corporation, or government agency—who damages another's person or property has wronged him, and a whole branch of Law covers wrongful acts, known in the profession as "torts." This was designed over the centuries to provide redress because, as one of the oldest and most frequently quoted rules of equity states: "No wrong is without a remedy." Finally, as we pointed out in Chapter 1, and as the rector and trustees of Trinity Church learned in 1895, the police power gives governments very large opportunities for regulating the use of property.

So why is it so hard to stop a paper mill from pouring its refuse into a river, or a mine from covering a pleasant landscape with acres of slag, or almost everyone from using internal combustion engines that poison the air? The reason is that for all our statutes and common law on the subject, a great deal of dirt remains legal.

One great source of this legitimate dirt is the vast accumulation from many small polluters. Each adds so little to the whole that none can be prosecuted seriously, or so most legislators and law enforcement people seemed to believe until recently. For example, more than three-fifths of all the contaminants in the air in the United States came from motor vehicles, according to a Public Health Service report in 1967. The total from this one source was 85,000,000 tons a year. All manufacturing, power plants, incinerators and other refuse burning, the heating of buildings and the other polluters put 48,000,000 tons into the atmosphere. Law now requires new automobiles to meet stricter standards than were even known a few years ago, but the increased use of cars and trucks keeps the total of their pollution at about the same level. Every ton of it is legal dirt. So is most of the refuse—gaseous, liquid, and solid—that pours forth from homes and factories, shops and offices, farms and camps, in fact anywhere people happen to be.

Nuisance law, which often seems the most obvious deterrent to such practices, has developed in response to public demand, but Law and people do not use the word in quite the same way. Law takes the first dictionary meaning—harm or injury. Popular speech prefers the secondary definitions—an annoying, unpleasant, or obnoxious thing or practice, a pest. Furthermore, Law recognizes two types of nuisance, public and private, and so many ramifications that William Prosser, when dean of the University of California Law School, warned that there is "perhaps no more impenetrable jungle in the entire law than that which surrounds the word 'nuisance.'"

Generally speaking, a private nuisance is a thing or practice that does damage to the person or property of an individual. Only he can sue to stop it. A public nuisance harms the community as a whole, not necessarily everyone in it but a substantial number. Only the public can sue to have it eliminated. A public nuisance may be a crime; a private nuisance is only a civil offense.

Most serious widespread pollution is by its nature a public nuisance, and Law has been slower to act against it than against private nuisances. Many states have spelled out in statutes certain specific nuisances, but some of their courts have held that giving a thing a bad name is not enough; it has to be a nuisance in fact, and the legislature's label is not a fact. So every nuisance suit has to be tried out for size, so to speak, and if the facts warrant, the courts permit states to add a nuisance to the rolls in the exercise of their police powers. Smoke, for instance, was not a common law nuisance. But in 1911, Iowa by statute gave smoke-abatement powers to cities of more than 65,000 people. Des Moines took advantage of this to prohibit dense smoke in certain portions of the city as a public nuisance. A lot of users of coal complained that the standards set were so strict that virtually all the furnaces in the affected districts would have to be remodeled. Their cries of anguish eventually reached the Supreme Court under the heading of *Northwestern Laundry v. City of Des Moines.*

The laundry company called the delegation of authority to mere commissioners unconstitutional because it deprived furnace owners of "due process of law," which the Fourteenth Amendment forbids. The due process clause is admittedly and no doubt purposefully vague. The lawyers for Northwestern Laundry said that surely it meant more than a rule promulgated by a board. They also contended that the Iowa statute permitted discrimination between coal users in different parts of the city and was both "unreasonable" and "tyrannical." On January 10, 1916, the Supreme Court unanimously rejected the argument, saying:

"So far as the Federal Constitution is concerned, we have no doubt the State may by itself or through authorized municipalities declare the emission of dense smoke in cities or populated neighborhoods a nuisance. Nor is there any valid Federal constitutional objection in the fact that the regulation may require the discontinuance of the use of property or subject the occupant to large expense in complying with the terms of the ordinance."

"No man can complain that he is injured by being prevented from doing to the hurt of another that which he has no right to do," a California court had expressed it in 1911, granting a permanent injunction against a cement company whose works impaired the value of adjacent residential property.

This seems clear enough, and *Northwestern Laundry* has been cited in suits to prevent pollution ever since. But courts have not always followed the doctrine literally. Fifteen years after the Supreme Court had spoken, a New York judge held in *Bove v. Donner-Hanna Coke Corporation* that the air pollution from fifty coke ovens was only a "petty annoyance." Bove, a home owner near the defendant's Buffalo plant, simply had to put up with it. The court called the smoke from these ovens "indispensable to progress." Of course, this was a lawsuit brought under the private nuisance theory. But the same company, taken into court in 1955 on a charge that the smoke from its plant, contaminating the same neighborhood, was a public nuisance, again escaped. This time the ruling was that the smoke was an "unavoidable necessity" because the coking ovens were equipped with every safeguard known to the industry. According to this court, coke is sufficiently important to the community that it must be permitted to exceed the pollution standards set by the government. About the same time, a Michigan judge rejected this plea of necessity, saying: "All it costs is money."

When Congress considered the point in writing the Air Quality Act of 1967, it leaned toward the New York opinion. In enforcing the standard of purity sought by the statute, the courts may consider "the technological (or physical) and economic feasibility" in deciding what "the public interest and the equities of the case may require." Although this was omitted from the original version of a successor act of December 1970, giving the Environmental Protection Administrator greater powers to enforce Federal water-quality standards, a new phrase was inserted during the legislation's peregrination through Congress. This tacked onto the enforcement provisions the words "taking into account the practicability of compliance." These are loopholes large enough to justify any pollution that a sympathetic judge is willing to allow.

Such an escape for perpetrators of a private nuisance is impossible, but then the successful litigant seldom protects anyone except himself. For example, as long ago as 1886 a New Yorker named Cogswell sued to force the New York, New Haven & Hartford Railroad to move an engine house it had built next to his home. He brought evidence to show that the noise and dust had made his son ill. The state courts agreed with the railroad's lawyers that each member of society must submit to "annoyances consequent upon the ordinary and common use of property." But the opinion added this phrase, "provided such use is reasonable." Using land next door to a residence for an engine house is not reasonable.

Law thus managed to distinguish an engine house from the rest of the railroad's operations and equipment. If tracks were laid only out of earshot of human habitations, people could not be served. Yards must be placed pretty much where traffic dictates. But the railroad can put its engine house where it does not unduly disturb residents who were there first. Even so essential a service as a railroad must be "reasonable."

Halfway across the country in 1969, the principle was applied similarly in *Bates v. Quality Ready Mix*. The defendant made a popular cement and had set up a plant on property it bought well out of town. It adjoined on two sides the land on which the Bates home stood, and the plant itself was 270 feet from the Bates house. The operation was exceptionally noisy and dusty, and went on day and night. Trucks came down the road at all hours to dump large quantities of dry materials that were then hoisted to a tank high in the air and mixed by machinery so incessantly deafening that the foreman bellowed his orders through a bullhorn. The finished product was loaded on other trucks and carted off with hardly less noise and dust. Even when the Bates family kept all their windows shut, dust and din came through to interfere with their sleep, conversation, and comfort. While no one was actually ill, the company's use of the land was found unreasonable in view of the fact that the Bateses had been there first. To the plea that no one could manufacture ready-mixed concrete without dust and noise, the court replied that this simply meant the plant must be closed, and it was so ordered. The judge made clear that noise alone would have been enough to justify this ruling. He also asserted that a nuisance does not have to affect health, only reasonable enjoyment of property, to be eliminated by Law.

All this was to the good: the railroad moved its engine house and Quality Ready Mix, its plant to places where no one lived, and the pollution did no obvious immediate harm, which is a desirable way of ending a nuisance. But when the pollution comes down a stream or is blown miles away by wind, the remedy for the wrong is not so simple. Often the victims have no way of identifying the culprit. Or no single polluter or group of polluters may be responsible in the eyes of Law. Scores of factories in a dozen industries may poison a river. But no single plant, perhaps no single industry, contributes as much as the water could handle. The wronged person or group would have no one to sue.

Recourse in Law, therefore, becomes one of government regulation of the wastes generated. Recent years have seen a rash of statutes at all political levels to set standards for pollution and sometimes even to enforce those standards. Congress has passed half a dozen since 1960. Whether they will be any more effective than the one of 1895 requiring Army Engineers' approval of discharges into navigable waters remains to be seen.

The favorite method of regulation has been prohibition of certain objectionable activities except in areas where they would not offend citizens, or at least citizens who mattered. A long line of court decisions upholds the authority of states, counties and municipalities to pass and enforce zoning ordinances on grounds of aesthetics as well as health or convenience or to preserve property values. The first such rules were olfactory. Soapmaking, tanning, slaughter houses and the like, which generated evil smells, were banned from many neighborhoods even earlier than the original antismoke ordinance. However, on premises outside the ban, these factories were permitted to create whatever stench their owners deemed necessary. This was legal dirt.

For a long time, Law refused to disturb such owners in the enjoyment of their legal rights on their own land that either had been set aside for such pursuits or where the neighbors did not object. But this right was gradually reduced as big cities expanded into outlying areas once set aside for the pariah trades. The Supreme Court opinion usually cited by lawyers who wish to circumscribe such property rights still further is one written in 1915 by Justice Joseph McKenna in *Hadacheck v. Sebastian.*

The plaintiff was the proprietor of a brickyard. Once it had been located outside Los Angeles, but now it was within the city limits, and a new ordinance made it a misdemeanor to operate such a business in certain districts. The defendant was the chief of police, into whose custody Hadacheck had been remanded when he refused to stop making bricks. His plea to the Supreme Court was that no one lived anywhere near his yard when he bought the land in 1902. People knew before they moved in how much noise and dirt a brickyard created. His eight acres were worth $800,000 for making bricks because of the quality of the clay but only $60,000 as residential property. (Against this it could be pleaded that the surrounding land was virtually valueless—as it had been before the city expanded—unless the brickyard was removed, so the property owners stood to gain more than Hadacheck would lose.) Finally, he argued, the city could not turn a legitimate business into a nuisance merely by calling names. His lawyers knew the Supreme Court had ruled some years before that a livery stable as a legitimate business was not *per se* a nuisance, but it was within the police power of Little Rock, Arkansas, "to declare that in particular circumstances and in particular localities a livery stable shall be deemed a nuisance in fact and in law." However, the Hadacheck counsel replied, a livery stable could be moved while a brickyard had to remain with the clay.

Justice McKenna pointed out that over the years the neighborhood had become residential, for whatever reason, and that "fumes, gases, smoke, soot, steam and dust arising from the petitioner's brickmaking plant have from time to time caused sickness and serious discomfort to those living in the vicinity." Even though Mr. Hadacheck was there first, the only limitation on the police power was that it not be used "arbitrarily or with unjust discrimination," which Los Angeles had not done. The justice neatly turned against Mr. Hadacheck the argument of many polluters that what they do is part of our advancing civilization. He wrote: "There must be progress, and if in its march private interests are in the way they must yield to the good of the community." Furthermore, Justice McKenna did not think the case so different from that of a livery stable, for Hadacheck could take the clay from his eight acres and make bricks elsewhere.

Hadacheck v. Sebastian and the many cases after it served to concentrate the obvious legal dirt where it would be relatively unnoticed or unobjectionable. But a great deal of dirt was not obvious, and in the absence of proof of damage, it remained legal everywhere. New York City incinerators, for example, routinely poured about fifty pounds of dust into the air for every ton of refuse burned. By the time a local ordinance set a limit of five pounds a ton, effective in December 1968, the total dust in the New York region from this single source was 15,000 tons a year. In the city, the excess over five pounds was legal until the new law went into effect. Most of the millions of tons of pollutants from our automobiles and trucks are legitimate, although new cars are obliged to be a little cleaner than the old ones—at least for the first few thousand miles. New

York City is still within the law when it empties a million gallons of raw sewage into its rivers every day.

Law is more effective if it deals with these problems at the source—the car manufacturer or the government of a city—than if it tries to arrest everybody who litters the streets. Either way, though, she first must end the dirt's legal sanction.

Cleaning the good ship Earth is, like peace, an ideal to which almost everyone subscribes. Yet the ideal falls so far short of realization that year by year the world gets dirtier. People cling to their own particular ways of fouling the common nest while deploring the other fellow's. Most of us drive our cars more rather than less. The uses of paper increase, although its manufacture is one of the foulest of industrial processes, and the final product adds up to half or more of the solid wastes in any large city. Americans who enjoy a day in the country burn forests, pollute streams, destroy nesting and feeding grounds of the animals they come to see, and leave a trail of garbage wherever they pass. Science has given them the means to do all this and much worse. Whether Science can reclaim what already has been destroyed is doubtful. There is hope that it may learn how to redress some of the wrongs technology has loosed. If it does, Law can help or hinder, whether the problem concerns the land, the water, or the air. Each of these three poses its own particular legal dilemma.

8 | Water,
Water Everywhere . . .

Anyone who dirties a water supply is so obviously offensive that one might suppose Law would regard the act as a wrong if not a crime. But in fact Law is schizoid on this point. Sometimes she seems to take the position of most people that a little bit of dirt never hurt a great big body of water. In other moods, because men are so dependent upon water for drinking, power, irrigation, and transportation, she has developed a vast amount of statutory and judicial regulation. These often vary with the different interests and needs of the societies that developed them. Arid states in the West and moist states in the East have quite different codes. This diversity is as great on pollution as on anything else, and understanding of Law in this field is complicated by her inability to reach very clear conclusions as to what "pollution" means. In fact, at times one suspects she has no certain definition for "water" either.

One of her problems is that Science frequently has no answer to the simple question. "Just how much does this process or practice foul the water?" (The same is true of air and soil pollution too.) Seldom if ever is a new technological advance postponed to determine what eventual side effects it might have on the environment. Law has not reached the point of holding, as Senator Edmund S. Muskie, for one, suggested about the discharge of wastes from any source: "You've got to take the point of view that if we don't know enough, we don't know enough to permit the discharge." Taken literally, that point of view would have delayed indefinitely the production of nuclear power and a host of common household and industrial products now taken for granted.

Nearly all water that anyone worries about is public property. Everything navigable—rivers, ports, the Great Lakes, etc. —is controlled by the Federal government. Since the 1899 Rivers and Harbors Act, the Army Corps of Engineers has been the agency chiefly responsible for them. Other streams that Law calls "meandering" and lakes that are not completely within a proprietor's own land are subject to the rules of the states. People on the banks have varying rights, depending on the state, but the general rule is that they cannot do anything to or with the water that adversely affects the people downstream or across the lake. Neither legislatures nor courts have spelled out just how adverse the effects have to be before Law steps in. Even wastes that clearly poison the water have been permitted—or at least Law does not prevent them—until once-pure rivers and lakes became no better than open sewers.

At last, accelerating damage from an accumulation of technological offenders, and the scientific proof of that damage, is moving Law to protect the water while something remains to be saved. Public demand for such action has proved so strong that Law has forced even the biggest sacred cow of our time, the high-speed automobile highway—that monster created in the name of progress—to yield at least once to a waterway. The damage feared was no threat to health or safety but to what one of the judges who heard the case called "scenic, historical and recreational values." The body of water rescued in this instance was the Hudson River.

Many New Yorkers, including the state legislators who set up a Hudson River Valley Commission to "encourage preservation, enhancement and development of the scenic, historic, rec-

reational and natural resources of the Hudson Valley," believed
that Law already had assured this result. But the Commission
was also charged "to encourage the full development of the
commercial, industrial, agricultural, residential and other resources." So when, in 1968, the New York Department of
Transportation submitted to the Commission plans for a six-
lane expressway that would run for ten miles on land to be
filled in along the east bank for as much as 1300 feet out from
shore, the Commission issued a "finding" that the project
"would not have an unreasonably adverse effect on the scenic,
cultural, recreational, or historic resources."

The commissioners may have been influenced by the fact
that the east bank of the Hudson in this area—from the New
York Thruway bridge across the river at Tarrytown to Croton-
ville—is hardly a beauty spot. The Penn Central Railroad runs
along the waterfront, and a great many drab industrial and
commercial buildings line the tracks. But it can be argued that
adding one eyesore to another was not the purpose of the act
creating the Commission. Two organizations, the Citizens
Committee for the Hudson Valley and the Sierra Club, plus
three residents in the area, took that position. They sued in
state court to have the Commission's findings set aside and the
Department of Transportation enjoined from proceeding with
the expressway. They lost, the judge virtually branding their
objections as mere quibbles.

The expressway also needed the consent of the Federal
government, and on January 27, 1969, after the state case was
decided, the New York Department of Transportation obtained
from the Army Engineers and the Secretary of the Army a permit for a dredge-and-fill operation that would dump 9,500,000
cubic yards of rock and dirt into the Hudson. A rock wall was
to keep the fill from sliding out into the middle of the river. The
plans called for this made land to be connected to the bridge
approaches at its southern end by a causeway. Whereupon, the
Citizens Committee and the Sierra Club, joined by the Village

of Tarrytown but without the residents, went into Federal court to stop the expressway. They chose procedural and technical grounds rather than an attack on the Engineers' judgment. The defendants now were the secretaries of the Army, Transportation, and Interior, the chief of Army Engineers, and the commissioner of transportation for New York.

The Citizens Committee and the Sierra Club, acting as "private Attorneys General," really wanted the expressway forbidden because they believed it would impair the scenic and other noneconomic values of the river, but they argued this only indirectly. Tarrytown said the village would lose money because of lower property taxes. But the main thrust of the argument was that the Army Engineers, and indeed the whole Executive Branch of the government, were without authority to permit such an expressway unless Congress specifically approved. The defendants not only denied this but protested that the plaintiffs had no standing to sue because they were not hurt yet. The committee and the club had "no personal economic claim to assert," and Tarrytown's property values could not be reduced merely by the excavation and fill but only when a road was put on top. The Federal officials also held that the decision as to a balance between beauty and utility, between nature lovers and motorists, rested in their hands. Finally, the government lawyers contended, a District Court has no jurisdiction to review a decision by the Secretary of the Army.

Judge Thomas F. Murphy had no trouble in allowing that the committee, club, and village had standing to sue. Less than three years earlier, the Scenic Hudson Preservation Conference had won its right to question the Storm King project only a few miles away on the other side of the river, with almost exactly the same interests to show as those of the committee and club. The village was right to enter the case at this stage, for if it waited until the state had gone to the enormous expense of those millions of tons of fill, it would be too late to halt even an illegal project. As to jurisdiction, he pointed out that while the court was not authorized to review specifically the Secretary's decisions, these fell within a general statute permitting suits that questioned "final agency action for which there is no other adequate remedy." The judge also noted that the Supreme Court had interpreted this to mean that jurisdiction over complaints involving Federal agencies should be restricted "only upon a showing of 'clear and convincing evidence' of a contrary legislative intent," of which no suggestion was introduced on behalf of the Secretary of the Army.

All this was prologue. It hardly touched on the issue at stake: whether the Army Engineers had exceeded their authority in granting the permit. When arguments did reach the main point, both sides relied upon the wording of the Rivers and Harbors Act of 1899. Each cited a different section. For the government, the key sentence read ". . . it shall not be lawful to excavate or fill [in a navigable waterway] unless the work has been recommended by the Chief of Engineers and authorized by the Secretary of the Army." The plaintiffs called attention to a previous passage which provided that when a bridge, dam, dike, or causeway was involved, "the consent of Congress" was also essential. (Later legislation gave advance congressional consent to any bridge approved by the Army Engineers and transferred causeways to the Secretary of Transportation, but dams and dikes were still covered.)

The point of law narrowed then to whether the permit issued was only to excavate and fill, which was within the sole jurisdiction of the Army, or also for a dike, which would need the consent of Congress. The government found a definition of "dike" in a technical dictionary first published forty years after the Rivers and Harbors Act was passed, which limited "dike" to "a wall . . . built as training works for a river so as rigidly to confine flow within definite limits." The expressway wall was not anything like this. However, as Judge Murphy pointed out, the Engineers had actually called that wall a dike several times in their permit. He also quoted newer dictionaries as defining "dike" as an embankment to control or hold back water or to serve as a barrier, which was obviously the intention here.

The Murphy decision granting an injunction against the project was handed down on July 11, 1969. It was confirmed on every point the following April by a three-man Court of Appeals in an opinion that went a little deeper into the real concern of the suing conservationists—what the expressway would do to the river. The three judges did not say just how much weight Army Engineers had to give to fish and wildlife conservation, pollution, aesthetics, and ecology. But they pointed out that various regulations required the Engineers to evaluate all of these as "relevant factors" before granting a permit. The plaintiffs had argued in both District and Appeals courts that the Corps had "arbitrarily and capriciously" ignored these factors.

The judges, having ordered the project stopped because it involved a dike that needed congressional consent, declined to consider the more difficult problem of the expressway's full effect upon the river. The appeals judges mentioned beauty and the rest only in connection with the standing of the committee and club. The concern of the two organizations for these factors, "apparent from the considerable expense and effort they have undertaken," gave them the right to sue. Whether they were correct in their appraisal of the damage that the expressway would do, the judges did not say.

The practical effect of the decision was to end plans for the expressway in the Hudson River, for on December 7, 1970, the Supreme Court refused to review. Any attempt to push an authorizing bill through Congress would clearly meet more public opposition than either house would care to encounter. So on the philosophical side, it could be considered that Law's ruling in favor of a river against a high-speed road is a triumph of conservation over technology. But a skirmish is not a war. Indeed, those who want to know just what Law requires of the Army Engineers in the way of preserving a river's natural state are no better informed than they were before the expressway was planned.

Older and more persistent than efforts to enlist Law in the protection of beauty has been the crusade for purity. Legislatures and courts have spun off thousands of statutes and opinions designed to prevent or correct water pollution by individuals, corporations, or public agencies. Both civil and criminal procedures have been invoked against the householder who throws his garbage into a lake, the company that spills or leaks oil into a harbor or offshore drilling site, and the municipality that releases raw sewage into a river. Lack of enforcement rather than lack of Law accounts for much of the pollution that persists. Also, many statutes that set standards exempt existing homes or factories or sewage systems or allow them a long time before they need stop.

Some contaminants were not known when the laws were passed and so are not always covered. Twelve thousand chemicals that have toxic effects in water are now used in industry. Five hundred new compounds are introduced every year. Inspectors of water supplies usually find out about the new ones only after they have been getting into water for years. The Federal Bureau of Water Hygiene in 1970 surveyed 969 systems ranging in size from that of New York City to rural Vermont. Of the 18,000,000 people served, about 2 percent were drinking water "of a potentially dangerous quality" because of disease bacteria and toxic metals. Many more of the thousands of samples taken showed amounts of various chemicals higher than the Federal standard but not yet dangerous to human health. However, some accumulate in gradually increasing amounts because they do not dissipate in water, and treatment plants often are not equipped to deal with them.

At the present stage of Law and Science, strict enforcement of all the regulations promulgated to clean the nation's waters would bring industry to a halt. The dilemma can be seen quite plainly in the legal history of just one of the best known chemical polluters, dichloro-diphenyl-trichloroethane, DDT, the insecticide hailed as a savior and damned as a destroyer within a span of two decades.

It was put together in Germany in 1874, but not until 1939 did Paul Mueller of Switzerland discover that it killed insects carrying disease, and thereby won the Nobel Prize. During World War II, DDT was dusted over millions of dirty people —soldiers coming out of combat and refugees herded into crowded camps. Then it was sprayed to kill malarial mosquitoes and pests that infest crops or cattle. Enthusiasts predicted a world free from every deadly or unwanted pest from houseflies to Japanese beetles.

Rachel Carson's *Silent Spring* shattered that fond illusion in 1962. One of the rare books that has changed the practices as well as the thinking of its readers, it explained dramatically why the effects of DDT and other miracle pesticides that Science was discovering were less than Utopian. For the first time, the public learned a few deadly facts about DDT. Its poisons, so effective against insects, kill other animals, too, once they get inside the body. The poison builds up (perhaps for years), collecting in organs that are rich in fats such as the liver or kidneys. Animals die from it because they eat other animals that have absorbed DDT or plants sprayed with it. Bees get killed along with the flies and mosquitoes, and species of flowers that rely on bees for pollination die out. The chemical is virtually indestructible. Insoluble in water, it is carried by rain and ground water into streams and lakes, passing from grub to fish, from berries to birds, from hay to cows. Miss Carson and her successors traced the devastation of whole areas of once pleasant countryside to DDT.

Four years after *Silent Spring*, in 1966, DDT inspired formation of one of the first organizations to engage man's pollution of nature in legal combat. On April 25, a 31-year-old Long Island lawyer, Victor J. Yannacone, filed what is called a "class" action against the Suffolk County Mosquito Control

Commission. On behalf of his wife Carol and all the other people in the county, although he had not asked most of them, he demanded that the Commission be enjoined from spraying DDT on local marshes because one of the effects was to kill fish in a lake. He called an ecologist, a biologist, and an ornithologist as expert witnesses. They so impressed Judge Jack Stanislaw of the County Court that he issued a temporary injunction on August 15. After hearing testimony and arguments for six days, he kept the injunction in effect for a year before he withdrew it, then reinstated it when Yannacone demanded further hearings. Finally the judge withdrew it again, ruling that although DDT was harmful to wildlife, the Commission was justified in using it for the protection of people.

Meanwhile Yannacone, with some of his witnesses and other interested individuals, had incorporated the Environmental Defense Fund. In November 1966 they undertook their second legal crusade against the Michigan Department of Agriculture, which was preparing to spray from the air to get rid of Japanese beetles on orchards located in Lake Michigan's watershed. The chemical to be used was dieldrin, which is about fifty times as toxic for birds and small animals as DDT. The State Court of Appeals at Grand Rapids granted a preliminary injunction but vacated it after a six-hour hearing on the ground that the Department had not exceeded its authority.

The Environmental Defense Fund has been joined as a legal gladiator by a number of other organizations committed to protecting water, air, and land from man and machine. More significant than the cases they win in court is the impetus they give to a public demand for more vigorous law enforcement and for the adoption of new legislation to block loopholes. The approaching end of the DDT story illustrates this point too.

First of all, Federal rules on use of pesticides grew stricter, requiring more explicit warning of danger and then imposing actual restrictions on spraying. By early 1970, the United States Department of Agriculture, which then regulated DDT, ordered no more spraying of tobacco fields, marshy areas or lakes, and around homes. Officials spoke of a possible complete prohibition. The Environmental Defense Fund did not drop its court action. On May 28, 1970, the U.S. Court of Appeals for the District of Columbia found for the Fund in two DDT suits. One commanded the Secretary of Agriculture to halt the registration of DDT for any shipment across state lines or give reasons for not doing so within thirty days. The other ordered that a proposal to forbid the spraying of DDT on any farm produce that was consumed raw should be published in *The Federal Register*.

A few days later, the Fund won without court action a suit that it, the National Audubon Society, and the National Wildlife Federation had brought against the Army, the Corps of Engineers, and the Olin Corporation. Olin manufactured about one-fifth of all the country's DDT in buildings leased from the Army at the Redstone Arsenal outside Huntington, Alabama. Wastes from this plant, flowing to the Wheeler National Wildlife Refuge, contained more than the allowed ten parts of DDT per billion parts of water, it was charged. Some animals in the refuge were said to have been found with lethal accumulations of the chemical in their tissues. Before the suit was brought, the Federal Water Quality Administration, a new agency created by Congress to set and perhaps enforce standards of purity, had recommended that the standard be twenty parts per trillion of water. This the Army rejected on the ground that Olin was reducing the amount of DDT in the waste as fast as it could. The three conservation organizations argued that this was not good enough, and their court action followed. On June 8, before it came to trial, Olin decided to close down the plant altogether, issuing a graceful statement saying that continued operation would not be consistent with the company's own ecological policy.

The legal fight on DDT moved onto the broadest possible national scene—the Fund still among the litigants. It was in on a "private Attorneys General" suit to compel the Environmental Protection Agency, recent successor to the Agriculture Department as regulator of DDT, to institute at once the steps necessary to bar DDT from interstate commerce. On January 6, 1971, a Federal court in Washington issued such an order, and the agency announced that it would not seek an appeal.

The fight over DDT led to wider airing in public of many other insecticides, herbicides, fungicides, and other new killers devised by technology to get rid of unwanted life. The public interest has been excited when one of them also kills or cripples human beings, as occasionally happens in peaceful application of the chemicals. Stricter legal regulation of civilian use is urged on the ground that these tragedies prove mere warnings on a label, or technical instructions accompanying a deadly drug to be placed in the hands of a farmer who reads at a third-grade level, if at all, are grossly inadequate. A mild remedy, which had the backing of President Nixon in February 1971, would forbid distribution of the more destructive pesticides, except on a restricted basis to authorized and trained personnel or by permit specifying the amount to be sprayed, the area to be covered and the precautions taken.

Law also seems to be bending in the direction of more work for the courts in protecting the environment. A Michigan statute of 1970 authorizes citizens to sue any body, state agency or private industry, that endangers natural surroundings or is not carrying out its legal obligations to protect the public from polluters. Copied by other states and adopted by Congress, this statute would place on the courts the burden of deciding not only when regulations are too oppressive, which they do now, but when the rules are too lenient or neglected altogether. The discretionary actions of regulating commissions or administrators would then be argued before judges, instead of at hearings conducted by the very individuals whose discretion is questioned.

Already such legislation as that initiated by the Environmental Defense Fund and others, the criminal proceedings possible under the Refuse Act of 1899, and the more leisurely regulations of the Water Quality Act of 1966 and its successor clarify Law's position. An Environmental Policy Act of 1969 requires every Federal agency that proposes activities or legislation affecting water resources, the air, or the land to describe these effects, evaluate them, and explain what alternative methods might accomplish the same purpose. The Clean Air Act of 1970 instructed the Environmental Protection Agency to study and comment upon each such agency statement.

As a practical matter, however, we should not expect too rigid enforcement until technicians come up with improved methods for disposing of industrial and agricultural wastes. Until then, the more outrageous offenders may be curbed, but the steady deterioration of fresh water in America will continue. It is significant that the victories over DDT seem to be possible only because even more effective pesticides, some of them more dangerous to people, are freely available. To create the kind of pressure that would stop pollution in the present state of Law and Science, Americans would have to take a long step away from the transportation, packaging, mechanical and electrical devices, and general comfort they now enjoy.

A way out of the impasse, in which Law would have a key role, is to prod Science to devise clean ways of producing cheap power, clean industrial processes, and manageable waste-disposal systems that do not simply transfer the pollution problem from air to water or water to soil. A statute taxing paper mills and all the other industrial polluters enough to pay for a clean-up job would inspire intensive search for cleaner methods of manufacture, or a substitute product—or make paper so expensive that we would use a great deal less of it. If everything now packaged in paper, cans, and bottles could be done up in something as ideal as that perfect container, the ice cream cone, our water would be much cleaner. The mountains of refuse pouring from big cities into rivers, lakes and seas have already spurred a technological search for recycling methods that will put the stuff to good use and keep it out of the garbage can.

Science would have to take the lead, even if Law provides the prod. If all or even many of the manifold technological dangers are to be ended and avoided, scientists would have to man what R. Stephen Berry in the *Bulletin of Atomic Scientists* has called "strong, well funded, and highly directed task forces to solve specific technical problems of environmental management." The soap industry's ability to change its product to meet the excessive perils found in detergents, described in Chapter 1, is an example of what Science can do—and an object lesson on the need for eternal vigilance to make sure it gets done.

A similar success in other industries could enable Law to operate more effectively than it now does. Prosecutors at all levels of government who are inclined to exercise their ingenuity to avoid applying current statutes and regulations to major offenders, the offenses being apparently unavoidable as well as common, would be more likely to crack down. At least they would lose the excuse for not doing so. We would encounter less need for the "private Attorneys General" attack because the official attorney general would not be so likely to falter. We see today that Law can discourage as well as forward these citizen court actions, as when the Internal Revenue Service rules that the lobbying and litigation expenses of those who try to keep the privilege of pollution are tax exempt, but the same expenses of organizations fighting the privilege are not. The rationalization appears to be that defense of pollution is a proper cost of doing business, but the nonprofit groups who would end pollution do not have any business.

Law is often only a paper tiger when she does confront really big polluters. This is nowhere illustrated more clearly than in the failure of a host of Federal and state enactments to protect the seacoasts from oil. If all of them were obeyed in letter and spirit, the periodic fouling of beaches and coastal waters could hardly continue. From the dribs and drabs of small pleasure craft to the Navy's deliberate dumping of half a million gallons at a clip, the rules are ignored—the Navy even professes itself to be above rules. Offshore drilling continues merrily, although a leak off Santa Barbara that drew nation-wide attention and condemnation when it began was continuing more than two years later and was still going on as this is written. In the Gulf of Mexico, joy has been expressed when a leak could be spouted into the air and the oil burned in fires lasting for weeks. At least this did not foul the water. One company was indicted, although it is not clear how its offenses differed from those of others, but the case has not been tried. The legal theory that the polluter can be made to pay for clean-up founders on the dismal fact that the oil cannot be cleaned up completely.

Multiply the oil problem by a couple of hundred others that imperil water and the Herculean task facing Law and Science is clear. It is a hopeful portent that although on the record Hercules was not unduly bright, he performed his labors successfully in the end. Like him, Law and Science have muscle.

9 | Air for Breathing

One of the by-products of modern technology is air that blisters paint, corrodes metal, and wilts plants. Science has been able to identify these poisons in the air we breathe and measure them with great accuracy, but is not quite so sure what they do to your lungs. Nothing good, the experts agree. They debate how many people are killed or damaged by air pollution, and the figure is large enough that in recent years a number of cities —Los Angeles the first—have begun through Law to reverse the trend toward choking their people with the fumes of progress.

So far, citizens' groups have initiated comparatively little litigation to stop major offenders or oblige government agencies to take action. Occasional individuals sue to get a specific nuisance eliminated when it affects them directly, and sometimes they win. But those seeking protection or preservation of the environment have failed either because they could not establish standing in court or were unable to pin the pollution complained of on specific defendants.

Progress toward air fit to breathe has been made largely through legislation, the most effective being that passed by municipalities in self-defense, although since 1963 Congress has passed several acts looking toward eventual control of pollution. The Environmental Protection Agency has made a start toward executing them. Each step has been a minor miracle in the face of opposition from many of the managers and owners of industry and property whom city councilmen and congressmen would rather not offend. Fortunately, the pressure has often been countered by the demands of other managers and owners who are either more enlightened or whose businesses are less likely to suffer from controls. By 1970, the cause of clean air was sufficiently popular that producers of highly polluting products were doubling and trebling their remedial research and vying with each other for conservationist approval. They were publicizing their successes, such as lead-free gasoline, with the ardor usually reserved for advancing the pretensions of a new breath freshener or deodorant.

Law welcomes this because it needs the support of public opinion. But Law needs more since the public itself is the cause of a large share of air pollution, mainly in the course of heating its houses and driving its cars. These two activities account for a considerable majority of two of the most dangerous contaminants, sulphur dioxide and hydrocarbons. Most urban air, however, contains varying amounts of many other substances that it owes to modern technology. The same technology has developed delicate instruments and processes that can measure the contents of any given sample of air with relative speed. The instruments even detect chemicals that no one knew were there. The most common gases pervading cities, besides the two mentioned, are carbon monoxide, oxides of nitrogen, organic aerosols, fluorides, mercury, asbestos, beryllium, and sulphide, all of which imperil human health. Usually a substantial mixture of soot and dust, chiefly from smoke, goes along with the gases. The different combinations produce different effects, all of them unpleasant and, in sufficient concentration, dangerous.

Law's principal weapon in any attempt to keep a given

situation from getting out of hand is to set what Science believes at the moment to be a safe standard of emission for the various sources of pollution. First in California and then nationally, new automobiles were required to be equipped to reduce the polluting gases coming from their exhausts, and stricter standards are in the offing. Municipalities regulate the amount of dust that an incinerator or factory chimney may emit. Many prohibit the open burning of refuse altogether since this releases more contamination into the air than almost any other disposal method.

These measures are still tentative gropings toward rules that technology can meet and people accept. Obviously the regulations have not produced clean air in big cities. The new automobile does not remain new for long, and without careful and frequent tuning, the engine sends out increasing amounts of hydrocarbons. When New York City set a low-dust-emission standard for all apartment house incinerators, effective in December 1968, its own public housing projects were the largest single group that failed to meet the deadline. Devices that permit clean burning of rubbish are expensive, and the city said it could not find the money to obey its own rules. Meanwhile, private owners fought the regulation to the ultimate arbiter, the Supreme Court, which finally upheld the ordinance. Only then, two years after the supposed deadline, could enforcement begin.

This does not mean that offenders are necessarily defying Law. Most clean-air statutes have loopholes that allow for "physical and economic feasibility," as in the Federal Air Quality Act of 1967. In practice, this means that government agencies and courts will determine how much pollution will be considered the inevitable accompaniment of a given industrial process—how much smoke from blast furnaces or power plants, how much sulphur dioxide from an oil refinery. Because neither scientists nor lawyers are omniscient, it takes years to develop fair, enforceable standards, since no one can be quite sure how they will work until they have been tried over large areas for a long time.

The legal ramifications are well illustrated in the first case brought by the national government to stop a polluter, this one under the Air Quality Act's predecessor, the Clean Air Act of 1963. The suit was filed in Federal court in 1965; the Supreme Court upheld the ruling in 1970.

The case dates back at least to 1956 when the Bishop Processing Company of Bishop, Maryland, was enjoined by a local court from emitting "noxious, offensive odors." This was in line with precedents for outlawing bad smells that go back in England for nearly a thousand years. But it is an old maxim that circumstances alter cases, and many industrial polluters think they face just the circumstances that prove a need for whatever they may happen to be doing. The Bishop Company contended that its odors were an inevitable by-product of its business, the rendering of chicken and other animal parts or refuse into fertilizer and poultry feed. The plant, valued at $350,000 and employing forty persons, was just a little south of the Delaware border, and the fumes were as pervasive in Selbyville, located just over the line in Delaware, as in Bishop. The company ignored the local judge's order, although it did pay a $5,000 fine for contempt of court. Finally in 1965, under the Clean Air Act, the Delaware Air Pollution Authority called a meeting of state and municipal agencies in Selbyville. From this emerged a formal demand that the Bishop plant put a stop to the foul smells by September 1, 1966. In the absence of any signs of compliance, a hearing board met on May 17, 1967, as provided in the Act, and forwarded this finding to Health, Education and Welfare:

"The malodorous pollution consists of sickening, nauseating, and highly offensive odors which are pervasive in effect to the interstate Selbyville, Delaware–Bishop, Maryland area . . . endangers the health and welfare of persons in the town of Selbyville . . . adversely affects business conditions and property values and impedes industrial development."

On the basis of this report, Health, Education and Welfare issued an order of May 25 that the company should cease and desist to the extent of installing effective controls of the pollution not later than December 1, 1967. When that date passed with the stench from Bishop as bad as ever, the Department of Justice was asked to take the company to court.

Defense lawyers attacked the Clean Air Act as an unconstitutional attempt to control a purely local activity. They also contended that the odors are not pollution in the legal sense, that only tangible or visible impurities could be so considered. On July 16, 1968, Judge Roszel C. Thomsen rejected both arguments. He affirmed what the local courts had held a dozen years before—Bishop had to stop using manufacturing processes that did such outrage to the air of its neighbors even if it meant going out of business. The company appealed.

Meanwhile, the slightly more stringent Air Quality Act of 1967 had been adopted, and the Justice Department decided to tackle Bishop in its first prosecution under this legislation. Before the case came to trial, the owner of the plant finally filed a formal agreement to stop polluting Selbyville's air if the Delaware authorities would make a new declaration that the odors did, in fact, cross the state line. But still nothing happened, while the appeal from Judge Thomsen's ruling wound its way to the Supreme Court. There, on May 18, 1970, the justices decided to let the Thomsen ruling stand.

By then, the 1967 statute was proving unsatisfactory to nearly everyone. The automobile industry was protesting a Health, Education and Welfare move to require 1980 cars to emit no more than ten percent of the carbon monoxide and sulphur dioxide released by the 1970 models. Conservationists were denouncing the delay until 1980, and other loopholes in the Act. As a result, Congress passed the Clean Air Act of 1970, and it was signed in December. Under its provisions, the Federal Government sets pollution standards through the Environmental Protection Agency, an independent executive body that took over the ecological functions of several departments. The states are required to submit their own plans for meeting these standards. If the EPA does not approve, it can impose its own plan. The process was designed to take a little more than a year to become effective after the Federal standards are promulgated. The EPA issued the first of them in the spring of 1971. The outlook is that enforcement will be left to states and localities unless Law decides to permit citizen intervention through class suits. This may lead to stricter standards than seemed likely in 1970. Two of the first states to act, Arizona and Montana, set stricter standards than the EPA.

Perhaps, in view of the leisurely pace of national cleansing devices, we should take comfort from the very real reduction in air pollution that Law has managed to bring about in less than a decade in certain industries in certain areas. When Los Angeles required all fuel oil burned within its borders to be not more than ½ of 1 percent of sulphur by weight, oil companies sued to have the order set aside. After a long fight, they lost in the county courts and, in January 1968, abandoned their appeal from that decision. By then, the effect of local ordinances on this and other industries was such that the assistant county counsel for Los Angeles estimated that the air was cleaner by 5,190 tons of harmful gases every day. His list was made up of organic gases, 1,230 tons; carbon monoxide, 1,945 tons; sulphur dioxide 1,445 tons; aerosols, 465 tons; oxides of nitrogen, 105 tons. In New York, recalcitrant landlords, who had resisted for three years the law demanding upgrading of incinerators finally lost their last appeal in the state's highest court at the end of 1970, and the Supreme Court refused to review that decision.

The significance of all this lies in the new direction that Law is giving to technology. Research departments that measured their success by speed and power and volume are being diverted to look for clean speed, purified power, and value rather than mass. If they do not find the antidotes to pollution, their companies may expect to become the targets for citizen suits, class actions, and tougher governmental law enforcement. The notion that automobile manufacturers might somehow be held accountable for the gases their cars loose upon us may take an even stronger hold on people, and therefore in Law, than it now has. Already a Federal judge has suggested that this is not impossible. While the case to which he addressed himself has not resulted in cleaner air, it suggests possibilities for future legal exploration.

The unlikely beginning of this particular anti-pollution move was an antitrust suit that the Department of Justice filed in January 1969 against the Automobile Manufacturers Association and the four major automobile producers. The government complained that the five had conspired to prevent or delay the development and use of equipment that would greatly reduce pollution by cars and trucks. However, the Department was not eager to press for a conviction, and the companies were understandably reluctant to have their affairs aired in court.

The real purpose of the suit was to prevent concerted procrastination by the industry in the future, and the industry was quite willing to forego such joint efforts. So a consent decree was acceptable to both parties. This legal device, a common solution in antitrust disputes, permits the defendants to agree that they won't do it again while not admitting that they ever did. In effect, they dodge the question, "Have you stopped beating your wife?" by replying, "I won't any more." The government is saved the task of proving a conspiracy, always difficult and often impossible even if it exists. The defendants are spared the risk of being found guilty, the onus of damaging testimony, and the expense of defending themselves although they may be innocent.

In this particular case, other litigants were more belligerent. They wanted to force the issue to court so that they could collect the triple damages that are authorized under the antitrust laws. But with the two principals satisfied with the consent decree, the interveners were declared to be without standing, and the matter was supposed to be closed.

Seven states, six cities, and an apricot farmer in California reopened it. They filed separate lawsuits in various Federal courts to force the companies to pay damages caused by their alleged conspiracy to delay the production of cleaner motor vehicles. The states and cities wanted their share of the eight billion dollars of damage that foul air causes every year. The apricot grower sued on behalf of all farmers whose crops are wilted by automotive fumes. At least one city, New York, also asked the court to order the makers to recall every one of their cars sold in the whole state and equip them with the latest exhaust controls.

To enable the courts to handle this rush of litigation, all the cases were lumped together for a hearing before District Judge Manuel Real in Los Angeles in September 1970. It was the first time that antitrust damages had been claimed by anyone who was not a customer or a competitor of the defendants. Lawyers for the manufacturers and the association argued persuasively, but not quite persuasively enough, that these novel claims should be thrown out summarily. Judge Real took the position that new knowledge of technological perils, such as exhaust fumes, has outmoded what he called the "traditional legalistic approach" and in effect makes new law. He found, therefore, that cities, states, and individuals had a right to try to prove their case. He implied quite clearly that he doubted they could do it, and indeed they have not so far.

The decision suggests that perhaps Law will open a way for the public to get into the clean air act without waiting for the slow process of legislation and enforcement. Judge Cardozo's revolutionary idea that Buick was responsible to MacPherson for the car it made, although he was not the company's customer, may inspire some other judge to hold Buick's successors accountable to the public generally for fouling the atmosphere. From the automobile, it is only a step to the big utilities, the blast furnaces, the metal refineries, and all the other individual polluters of the air we breathe.

10 | Air for Communicating

Almost from the moment men began to send messages through
the air without the help of wires, they found that they needed
Law to make the thing work. Without some legal authority to
say who could use which channels, everybody jammed everybody else, and no one received an intelligible message. Before
World War I, the wireless was mainly a marine service for
communication between ship and shore or ship and ship. It was
hardly a rival of the telegraph and cable companies in their
domain, but it was considered to be subject to the same legal
rules.

In 1912, Congress recognized its existence as a separate
legal entity, assigning the Department of Commerce to supervise commercial wireless and requiring all transmitters to have
a Department permit to operate. This worked well enough, especially as the Navy took over entirely for the duration of our
participation in the 1917–19 war. Then radio broadcasting into
the home in the early 1920's changed the industry from a pur-
veyor of messages to a major medium for getting news, entertainment, talk and advertising—lots of advertising—directly to
the consumer.

The growth of radio, and the growth of the problems it set
for Law, was furiously fast. In 1922, when *The New York*

126

Times began to list the offerings of stations that broadcast every day, it had to go as far west as Chicago to make up a list of six. The whole country boasted only 30 stations and 60,000 receiving sets. But in 1927, when a congressionally created Federal Radio Commission sought to bring a little order out of the chaos, it was difficult not to receive two or three stations at once because 733 of them were competing for the attention of the owners of 7,300,000 sets over 89 channels. Confusion had been compounded when in 1926 the Supreme Court held that existing laws did not permit Secretary of Commerce Herbert Hoover to cancel Zenith Radio Corporation's permit merely because its station used an unauthorized frequency. With rare promptness, Congress proceeded to plug this hole. Otherwise, the owners of those 7,300,000 sets would have heard nothing but inarticulate noise over the air, and no congressman wanted to face their anger if he let that happen. Already, the jumble was such the cynics were calling radio "air pollution," a term that many applied later to programs they did not like. When the full power that the owner of a license could wield became apparent, the phrase was changed to "a monopoly of air pollution." This power was so widely recognized that Congress stipulated no alien might own a broadcasting license.

The Radio Act of 1927 was based on the theory that the public owned the air not only for the passage of airplanes through it but as a medium for broadcasting. Therefore, every radio station using the public's air had to get a license from the new Radio Commission, at first good for only six months, then a year, and later three years. The Communications Act of 1934 established a new watchdog for the industry, with broader powers, the Federal Communications Commission. It also spelled out every station's duty to operate primarily in the public interest in return for the privilege of sending its programs and commercial messages through the public's air. The privilege already was so profitable that it was called "a license to print money."

The Supreme Court held, however, that the government did not grant any license in perpetuity. In two cases in 1931 and 1932, it confirmed the Federal authority to refuse license renewals. The first of these concerned KFKB Broadcasting Association, a name under which a vendor of patent medicine sold his wares by blatant misrepresentation over the air. The second was Trinity Methodist Church, the cloak for a somewhat unorthodox minister who combined violent abuse of his opponents with blackmail. The Radio Commission rejected their applications for permit renewals. Both claimed that the First Amendment guaranteed them the right to say what they pleased over their own stations. The Supreme Court held that the constitutional protection of free speech did not apply to their activities, and the Commission was within its rights in refusing to renew the licenses.

Despite these clear precedents, the FCC exercised its powers so mildly that in 1946, when it finally began talking about not renewing licenses of stations that failed to provide the public interest programs that the act of 1934 demanded of them, the president of the National Association of Broadcasters cried out that such a concept of public service "had no application to radio broadcasting." When the Commissioners actually did make some rules, the courts upheld their right to do so.

One reason for the slow pace was that Law entered unexplored legal territory when it began to regulate broadcasting. No other comunications medium used the public's own facilities. On the other hand, the idea of a government official telling anyone what he should or should not say to the public was repugnant to the spirit of the First Amendment. The Supreme Court found radio and the movies just as much part of the press that the Constitution said was free as were newspapers and magazines. Once that is conceded, the question remains as to just what limits Law places on the FCC's authority to dictate to broadcasters and on the stations' right to broadcast whatever they please.

Over the years, the courts have tended to increase the latitude allowed government in forcing the holders of licenses to live up to standards that meet the statutory obligation of "public convenience, interest or necessity," and at the same time to protect the broadcasters who take positions on public issues or offend by tasteless or denunciatory remarks. The most notable of the first was the prohibition of cigarette commercials as of January 1, 1971. A good example of the second was permission for stations to editorialize.

The cigarette advertising ban, on the ground that cigarettes are dangerous to health, was exceptionally severe action for the Commission to take against a major source of broadcasting revenue. But it had been presaged by ominous rumblings almost as soon as the first advertising was heard on the air. The American Telephone and Telegraph Company's New York City station WEAF broadcast the pioneering blurb on August 28, 1922, ten minutes of praise of a new cooperative-apartment development in the Borough of Queens. Before the year was out, Herbert Hoover, as Secretary of Commerce, called a meeting of broadcasters in Washington.

"It is inconceivable that we should allow so great a possibility for service, for news, for entertainment, for education, and for vital commercial purposes to be drowned in advertising chatter," he told them.

The broadcasters present so little foresaw their medium's potential for ballyhoo that they proposed to allow nothing more in the way of paid advertising than the mere name of whoever paid for a program. They were happy to make this gesture because profits for their new industry, they thought, would come from the manufacture and sale of sets. David Sarnoff, head of the Radio Corporation of America and father of the idea of replacing individual headsets with a box that the whole family could hear, had proposed earlier in 1922 that actual broadcasting be turned over to a nonprofit corporation or corporations. He suggested that programming should be endowed by philanthropists and perhaps involve a small royalty on sets. His view of the economics of radio was based on the fact that already RCA derived four times as much of its income from sets as from the sale of the wireless services for which it had been created. But by the time Hoover began his second term as Secretary of Commerce, in 1925, advertisers were in control of the medium, and they still are the principal source of revenue. It took the government twenty-two years after Hoover's first protest to warn the industry of possible losses of licenses if it seemed that a station was operated "solely in the interest of advertisers rather than of listeners." By then, the public was becoming a little restive, and the head of the Columbia Broadcasting System, William S. Paley, conceded that the industry was guilty of what he called "advertising excesses." The resulting voluntary restrictions on the volume of commercials, while far from satisfying the critics, kept Law off the broadcasters' backs until the cigarette controversy.

During the years of the cigarette debate, Science established to the satisfaction of most people that smoking is injurious to health. The first efforts to enlist Law against the industry were suits in which sufferers from lung cancer, or their survivors, sought damages from the companies whose brands the victims smoked. On this issue, the tobacco companies had Law on their side, a typical example being *Pritchard v. Liggett & Myers.* Otto Pritchard was a Pittsburgh cabinetmaker who concededly had smoked Chesterfield cigarettes, made by the defendant, from 1921 to 1953. That year he had to have a lung removed because of cancer. Five qualified physicians testified that the cancer was caused by smoking, and they were not contradicted at the trial. Pritchard claimed punitive as well as actual damages, since Chesterfield advertising, he asserted, warranted the cigarettes to be harmless. Sample advertisements over a period of twenty years were quoted—"Play Safe—Smoke Chesterfield," "Chesterfield is Best for You," and so on.

The maker's claim that most influenced judges was contained in commercials aired in 1952 by Arthur Godfrey, who himself contracted lung cancer later. The basis of these commercials was a report by Arthur D. Little, Inc., the leading research outfit employed by the tobacco industry. These declared flatly: "Nose, throat, and accessory organs not adversely affected by smoking Chesterfields." Godfrey himself remarked later in the broadcast: "That they mean what they say—that specialist said it, Liggett and Myers have substantiated it. Remember that when you are thinking about cigarettes. Smoke Chesterfields—they're good."

In spite of this, the Federal trial judge directed the jury to bring in a verdict for the manufacturer. He informed them that no breach of warranty was involved. He also seemed impressed by the company's argument that it was putting out a standard product no different from cigarettes made by others. Pritchard appealed, and the Court of Appeals ruled unanimously that the trial judge had erred. He should have left it to the jury to decide as to the warranty, the adequacy of the Little tests, and the company's obligation, if any, to warn smokers of their danger.

So the case went back to be tried all over again before the same judge in 1962. He told the jury to reach a verdict that would answer these questions: (1) Did smoking Chesterfields cause Pritchard's lung cancer? (2) Did Liggett & Myers give Pritchard any warranty on which he relied? (3) Was any implied warranty breached? (4) Did Pritchard assume the risk himself when he smoked Chesterfields? The twelve replied yes to the first and fourth questions but no to the others and agreed that Pritchard was not entitled to any damages at all.

The failure of this approach to ending or at least reducing the cigarette menace was succeeded by the war on cigarette advertising. By the time this was won, Law faced some questions that may take even longer to work out than the effect of smoking on health. Why should not the government forbid cigarette advertisements in the press? Has it more right in this area of

First Amendment privilege to control a licensed industry than one that is unlicensed? Is the supposed relative ease of starting a newspaper or magazine as against a broadcasting station a factor? (Actually the United States has nearly four times as many radio and television stations as daily newspapers.) Must the government ban all cigarette advertising if it bans any, as the tobacco industry has contended?

These questions have led to less legal argument than another aspect of regulation—the government's assertion that every licensee is obliged to broadcast all points of view. The best-known pronouncement of this kind is the requirement that a station must give equal time to all candidates for public office during an election campaign. Abrogated by an act of Congress expressly for the 1960 debates between John F. Kennedy and Richard M. Nixon, the "Fairness Doctrine" also has been used to give persons or organizations who have been attacked a chance to reply over the same station or network. No such obligation rests upon other media of communications—press or platform or pulpit—but this one is firmly lodged in Law on the premise that the air for all broadcasting purposes belongs to the public. Two cases of 1969 are now cited frequently as indicating the inviolability of this concept.

Red Lion Broadcasting Co. Inc. et al v. F.C.C. et al stemmed from a radio "sermon" delivered by the Rev. Billy James Hargis of the Christian Crusade. "The presidential election of 1964 had been decided only three weeks before, and the Reverend Billy, an ardent advocate of what he considered conservatism, was bitter against everyone who had contributed to the defeat of Barry Goldwater. On November 27, he used one of his series of broadcasts over station WGCB in Pennsylvania to denounce Fred J. Cook, author of a book entitled *Goldwater —Extremist on the Right,* as a worker for a Communist-affiliated newspaper, a defender of Alger Hiss, an assailant of J. Edgar Hoover, and now a smearer of Goldwater. Cook demanded free time to reply under the "Fairness Doctrine," and the station refused. The FCC ordered Red Lion, the owner, to grant the time; the Court of Appeals affirmed the order, and the Supreme Court agreed. By now it was June 8, 1969, a rather long time for a man to have to wait to answer an attack, since presumably most listeners had by then forgotten who said what about whom. But the point at issue was an important one in all the future communication uses of the air.

"It is the right of the viewers and listeners, not the right of the broadcasters, which is paramount," Justice Byron R. White wrote for the unanimous Supreme Court.

The company had asserted its right of free speech to criticize in its own way a writer who put his views before the public. The opinion noted this only to reject it, saying:

"No one has a First Amendment right to a license. There is nothing in the First Amendment which prevents the Government from requiring a licensee to share his frequency with others and to conduct himself as a proxy or fiduciary with obligations to present those views and voices which are representative of his community and which would otherwise, by necessity, be barred from the airwaves."

This was the Warren court speaking. That the Burger court would reverse this trend is unlikely. At the time of *Red Lion,* the present Chief Justice wrote his last opinion as a Court of Appeals judge in *Office of Communication of the United Church of Christ v. FCC.* The plaintiff was seeking the right to present evidence in a license-renewal hearing. Judge Burger's court ruled that the FCC was obliged to pay attention to what such organizations had to say. The soon-to-be Chief Justice added:

"By whatever name or classification, broadcasters are temporary permittees—fiduciaries—of a great public resource and they must meet the highest standards which are embraced in the public interest concept. The Fairness Doctrine plays a very large role in assuring that the public resources granted to licensees at no cost will be used in the public interest."

Such pronouncements have little serious effect upon what the public sees and hears on radio and television. As recently as 1967, the FCC ruled that 33 minutes of commercials per hour would meet the public-interest rule. One abortive attempt to bring the real arbiters of broadcasting content under the rule of Law exemplifies the difficulties. Survival of most major TV entertainment is largely determined by the various ratings that purport to reveal how large a proportion of viewers or listeners is tuned in to a given station at a given time. Three companies whose estimates mean life or death to a program are the American Research Bureau Division of C-E-I-R, Inc., the A. C. Nielsen Company, and The Pulse, Inc. On December 28, 1962, all three signed consent orders that they would "cease and desist" from representing that their measurements, expressed in figures as precise as one percent and even one-tenth of one percent, were anything but estimates. The companies agreed also to "cease and desist" from a variety of misrepresentations that gave a misleading impression of the accuracy with which they stated the size of an audience. The Nielsen order, for example, cited twelve such practices.

These orders, of course, were not an outright confession of wrongdoing. Yet the complaint under the Federal Trade Commission Act described violations of the statute that the companies did not answer. The Commission listed ten ways in which Nielsen "uses techniques and procedures that result in bias or error other than sampling error and which adversely affect the accuracy of its 'ratings' and audience 'totals.' " Similar findings were made about the other rating firms.

The frauds that the companies agreed to abandon are not the important issue from the standpoint of the average television viewer. He is concerned with the type of program he gets as a result of the estimates, and for helping producers decide what he wants, a bad poll is better than none at all. Law should be chiefly concerned that the facts of the sampling are presented in reasonably intelligible form so that if the errors are outrageous the public has a chance to make its voice heard. The alternative is probably pay television. Then the measurement of the audience would be the number of viewers who have paid, as is the case now with a newspaper or magazine. Identification of public desire becomes more vital to the public interest as the impact of materials broadcast to the minds of men becomes more complex and more influential.

At this stage of broadcasting's scientific development, the stand that Congress, the FCC, and the courts have taken in regard to it suggest how Law will look upon the transmission through the air of facsimile and video recording that can revolutionize banking and credit, newspapers, shopping, and education. The technology we already have, if put to full use, could make everything we say and do instantly available to Big Brother whether he is a government agency, a credit institution, or a well-heeled private snoop.

That technology can give us the opportunity of making our views known to government, or expose us to incessant propaganda and brainwashing. For instance, a laser tube about an inch in diameter can carry 100,000,000 voice channels. The ease and speed of inexpensive duplicating processes such as Xerox and home tapes, cassettes, and the rest open the books of all the world's knowledge to any student or teacher. These processes also complicate rights in literary property, so Law is grappling with new concepts. Should a teacher or librarian be allowed to duplicate any book or article for a class or other group without paying the author? Should they be allowed more without fee than an individual? More than a duplicator who sells the copies? Assuming that even teachers are not allowed to steal the author's work—the existing copyright laws suggest they may not—how big an extract would be exempt as fair comment? A whole chapter? A page? A paragraph? What system of payment should be required? A flat fee of so much a page, with the copyright office the collector and distributor of the royalties? Should authors, as some teachers and librarians suggest, be compelled to allow their works to be read and studied in an educational setting and waive any payment if each copying is less than, say, thirty or fifty copies? (Of course, this is not suggested by teachers and librarians who have written textbooks.)

All these technological problems combine to give Law—and the public, which can make Law when it wishes—a choice and an opportunity. She can open the air channels to the individual for speaking his mind or she can permit the state or licensed groups to control his mind.

When Law is obliged to weigh the risks and benefits of these coming uses of the public air, she may well rely on some precedents drawn from media other than broadcasting. One of the cherished liberties that have stemmed from the First Amendment is that a "free flow of ideas" (the Supreme Court's phrase) may never be blocked by government or anyone else. The right of an idea to be disseminated is more important in Law than the desires of the people who do the disseminating. The court expressed that point of view admirably in 1944 in *Associated Press v. U.S.*, a case that also exemplifies how our legal system turns a statute designed to correct one evil into a remedy for another.

The judges reached their conclusion about the traffic in ideas by way of the Sherman Antitrust Act, passed in 1890 to preserve competition among businessmen. In the Associated Press case fifty-four years later, the court was construing these words in the statute:

"Every contract, combination in the form of trust or otherwise, or conspiracy, in restraint of trade or commerce among the several States, or with foreign nations, is hereby declared to be illegal."

The Act also declared such contract or combination a crime, punishable by jail as well as fine. But that it applied to the collection and distribution of news as well as to deals in finance, industry and commerce was a very far-out notion until the government took a hard look at the way the country's leading wire service was organized. The Associated Press was in effect an exclusive club composed of member newspapers. No new member could be admitted except with the approval of all the other members in its city, which meant no new members at all. No nonmember could subscribe to or receive AP dispatches, which were so valuable that their AP franchise was the only marketable asset some newspapers had. When the suit was filed, even editors who generally approved of antitrust prosecutions cried out that the government was trying to undermine freedom of the press. (Editors and publishers often find it impossible to distinguish between freedom of the press and their own freedom to make money.) The Supreme Court, far from accepting this argument, pointed out that it was in the very interest of the constitutional safeguards surrounding a free press that the AP must sell its news service to any paper willing to pay for it.

"Surely a command that the government itself shall not impede the free flow of ideas does not afford nongovernmental combinations a refuge if they impose restraints upon that constitutionally guaranteed freedom," the opinion read. "Freedom to publish is guaranteed by the Constitution, but freedom to combine to keep others from publishing is not."

This is the principle that forbids broadcasters to exclude from the air opinions they do not like. Maintained by effective enforcement and public pressure, it should preserve the free flow of ideas through any and all of the new marvels of transmission.

11 | Air for Travel

The legal issues raised by commercial and military aviation were hardly settled for all time just because Congress appropriated the air for people to fly through in 1926 and a chicken farmer established twenty years later in *U.S. v. Causby* that this didn't really mean all the air (as mentioned in Chapter 2). Rather, the science of aeronautics asked a new question for every one that Law answered, and is still doing so.

As planes got bigger and faster and airports larger, the problems of adjusting the rights of dwellers on land to the needs of an expanding industry grew more difficult. Even people not directly under the path of the planes sued for damages and collected. But air traffic insatiably demanded new city airports before the public was accustomed to the noise and congestion of the old ones.

The first rule to meet this situation was enunciated by the Georgia Supreme Court in 1942 and incorporated in an act of Congress in 1958. It stipulated that airport builders should acquire enough land ahead of time so the traffic would not become a nuisance to the neighbors. Unfortunately, neither courts nor legislators nor engineers are very good at predicting how much land is enough. Airports retreated farther and farther from the hearts of the cities and spread over more and

138

more countryside, but their new neighbors complained as loudly as the ones they left behind. Judges had to decide how far objectors were justified and who should pay for the damage to property and comfort when they were.

Before solid precedents could be established, along came jet engines, and flight patterns that had been tolerable became offensive. What this technological advance should do to Law and Law to it was duly litigated, and on January 16, 1962, the U. S. Supreme Court was listening to arguments in *Griggs v. Allegheny County*. The nine judges were called upon to determine who is liable for damages when an airport's planners fail to make it big enough so that the "glide path" of incoming and outgoing jet aircraft does not unreasonably disturb those who live beneath it. The owner of the airport, said the opinion of the court, written by Justice Douglas, who had drafted *Causby* eighteen years earlier.

In this case, the owner was Allegheny County, which contains Pittsburgh, and its designers had laid out the Greater Pittsburgh Airport so that planes following the official flight pattern might come within twelve feet of the chimney on a house owned by a Mr. Griggs and never cleared it by more than 300 feet. Even with soporifics and earplugs, sleep was impossible, and the family had to move out. Griggs sued for compensation on the ground that the county had "taken" an easement on his property. The Court of Common Pleas awarded him $12,690, but the state Supreme Court said no, if there was a "taking" of the Griggs property, Allegheny County didn't do it. The implication was that the Federal government should hold the bag since under the National Airport Act it paid most of the bill for the Pittsburgh field.

Justice Douglas and all but two of his colleagues disagreed. A county agency had designed the facility, and it should have provided enough air space as well as enough solid land, and therefore should have bought out Griggs in the first place. A bridge builder must acquire sites for the approaches as well as those for anchoring the span, the opinion pointed out, and the builder of an airport has a similar obligation.

But what if you had enough land for all reasonable purposes until a new type of plane required more? This question was answered in *Highland Park v. U.S.*, a direct suit against the government permitted under Public Law 601, which allows the United States to be sued for damages on almost the same terms as anyone else. It was passed in 1947, so soon after the final *Causby* decision that some commentators thought it was a result. *Causby* had been decided on the basis of the Fifth Amendment that, besides its better-known safeguard against forced self-incrimination, forbids government seizure of private property without compensation. Public Law 601 not only widened grounds for collecting a claim but permitted a citizen who had been damaged to seek redress without making it a constitutional issue.

Highland Park, a residential community, had coexisted happily enough with a nearby Air Force field until jet bombers came along. Then noise and vibration became almost unbearable. Windows shook and dishes rattled; radio and TV reception was constantly interrupted; conversation was almost impossible. After several residents fell ill, the developer sued in the Court of Claims to recover the loss in value of his lots and houses. One of his bits of evidence was a government recommendation against building a school in the neighborhood because the jets made so much noise that teaching would be disrupted.

The defense replied that people who had never complained of airport noise before had no right to do so just because a new kind of plane was introduced. The residents were in the same legal situation as householders alongside a railroad. For one hundred years it had been sound law that the nuisance of passing trains, almost as noisy and in the early days a great deal dirtier than jet aircraft, was something the neighbors had to put up with in the interest of all the people who benefited from improved transportation. The legal principle is that the rights of a few will be sacrificed if society as a whole gains or is endangered. The right of free speech, for example, does not extend to yelling "Fire!" in a crowded theater. The rights of property must also yield to the greater good, and the government lawyers argued that the residents of Highland Park were in that position.

The Supreme Court rejected both arguments. It noted that it had already disposed of the railroad analogy in *Causby*. Furthermore, the jet planes did make a difference, so great that at the very moment the Air Force flew in its first jet, with the intention of doing it regularly, the government had taken some of the developer's property and would have to pay for it.

The decision was an important one in influencing builders of jet airports to buy up enough land to accommodate the noisier planes. It also serves as a possible warning for a future when even noisier or otherwise more objectionable flying objects than jets will begin using the public's air. The most likely problem of this kind to be posed for Law by aviation will be the supersonic commercial transport. Noise at the airport could be one of the least of the problems, and already we have an interestingly confused body of law for the legislators and the judges to ponder. Such bewilderment is not unusual when technology comes up with what Thoreau called "improved means to an unimproved end."

Up to the present, all supersonic flying in this country has been done by the armed forces. The results on the ground have been sufficiently destructive so that proponents of civilian craft of this type have promised to restrict the machines to transoceanic flights. No one knows what damage they might cause at sea. In developing new technology in the past, the principle of "what you don't know can't hurt you" prevailed. This has been the common practice in introducing new chemical processes in industry or, until recently, a new method of burning trash. So why not wait and see if supersonic airliners will damage the environment? In the actual debate, the more compelling arguments against such planes were their intolerable noise at takeoff and landing, even at subsonic speeds, and the enormous expense—billions of government money to subsidize fast flights for few people. (No one seriously suggested that the prospect of supersonic travel is sufficiently attractive for private capital ever to build the first planes.)

This hardly settled the future of supersonic travel. Technology, it is safe to say, is not so bankrupt that it cannot and will not reduce the noise level to that of present planes and protect the environment at the same time. Then the objection to government subsidy would lose a great deal of its force, since that has been the foundation of all transportation improvements since canal barges. Government underwrote railroads lavishly, paying the full cost and more of building many. It still subsidizes motor vehicles with billions of dollars' worth of highways, and aviation with airports. Once the supersonic airliner becomes commonplace in crossing the oceans, the demand for speed in crossing the continent will surely be met. When that time comes, the foreseeable legal problem will be the phenomenon known as sonic boom.

Law has had more experience with it than the arguments over whether or not to build a civilian test airliner would indicate. Perhaps this experience has been overlooked because the damage so far has been caused by military planes, and nearly all the claims have been settled—thousands of them—according to rules set up by the Army itself. No proof of negligence or wrongdoing is required. The Army investigates, mostly just to be sure a military plane broke the sound barrier in the vicinity of the damage at the time the damage was done, and that it was the sort that sonic booms can cause. Then the government pays claims up to $5,000 without further hearings. This takes care of the overwhelming majority of cases, which mostly involve cracked windows and plaster walls or scared animals— turkeys and chickens that dash themselves to death, ranch mink that eat their young, horses and cattle that cut themselves on fences.

More formal procedures are in order when the claims rise above $5,000. The injured citizen can either sue under Public Law 601 or try for a private appropriation bill that has to pass both houses of Congress and in practice must have the support of the Secretary of the Army. Both procedures are slow, and therefore property owners with large sonic-boom claims have tried to collect from their insurance companies. These cases, better than military settlements, suggest how Law might handle similar suits against commercial airlines.

One of the very first was brought by a contractor who was building a new control tower at Donnelly Field in Montgomery, Alabama. On May 18, 1958, a sonic boom twisted the aluminum ribs of the almost completed tower out of shape, tore away bolts, and flattened a temporary metal building nearby. The contractor asked his insurance company to pay for the damage under a usual "builder's risk" policy. The company refused, and *Bear Brothers Inc. v. Fidelity & Guaranty Insurance Underwriters Inc.* was filed in the state courts. The verdict hinged on whether or not a sonic boom is an explosion, which was covered by the policy.

The expert testimony was technical in the extreme, learned, and contradictory. After listening to it, the judge decided to accept the layman's idea that "the term explosion is commonly and ordinarily understood to mean a violent bursting or expansion, following the sudden production of great pressure as in the case of explosives or a sudden release of pressure as in the rupture of a steam boiler. An explosion occurs when there is an instantaneous release of pressure or instantaneous elimination of a pressure differential. . . . The Court is further of the opinion that 'sonic boom' is a new term which has not acquired a fixed meaning in the minds of the general public." On that basis, he ruled that a sonic boom was not an explosion and dismissed the claim. Bear Brothers appealed, but before the appeal could be heard, the government, which did not want to wait for its control tower while the case dragged on, paid for the damage.

Another case originating in 1958 got us a little further. A sonic boom demolished the four-story Alexander warehouse in Hico, Texas, and the Firemen's Insurance Company rejected a claim under a policy that promised to pay for loss "from explosion . . . or damage by aircraft." The company said a sonic boom was not an explosion and that "damage by aircraft" meant damage caused by something falling from it or being hit by it. The judge refused a motion on behalf of Alexander to instruct the jurors that sonic boom is an explosion. But he did instruct them that the destruction caused by a boom was "damage by aircraft" if they found that a plane caused the boom. Both sides were unhappy with this, and the Texas Court of Civil Appeals heard the arguments all over again. It upheld the trial judge, saying it didn't know what a sonic boom was—anyone who relied on explosion coverage would have to prove it by more convincing evidence than had been adduced—but it was caused by aircraft.

Even if the explosion definition becomes accepted, the victim of future sonic booms will be much better off in some states than others. The long-established law of explosions has developed differently among them, and legal authorities have suggested that the courts will look to the old "blasting cases" for precedents in sonic-boom damage. The suggested analogy is to a dozen cases or so of dynamite stored by a road or tunnel builder that go off through no fault of his (it happens often enough) and do serious damage to a house or people half a block away. No negligence is suggested, but dynamite is dangerous stuff, and a man who stores it is responsible for it in ways that would not apply to the same amount of flour.

In New York State the responsibility is limited. If the explosion hurled rocks and iron and wood onto the neighbor's property, that is a trespass and the neighbor can collect. But if the damage was done by shock waves, as frequently happens with dynamite and always with sonic booms, the blaster is not liable so long as he was on his own property and proceeding "with due care and without negligence." So said the state's highest court.

Connecticut's judges take a different view. They see no practical or logical difference between liability for damage caused by flying rocks and that resulting from shock waves—"in each case a force is applied by means of an element likely to do serious damage if it explodes." The quoted words are from an opinion of that state's highest court. More of the country follows Connecticut than adheres to the New York interpretation.

People who are injured in property or person by civilian supersonic transports will have to surmount a problem that does not face those who sue the military. They will have to establish whose plane set off the boom that did the damage. This might not be easy; the offender would be out of sight and going so fast he would be in the next state before the plaster stops falling or the wound begins to bleed. But assuming that Congress obliges the airlines to set up a pool to meet such contingencies or otherwise eliminated this difficulty, the plaintiff still would have some hurdles to overcome. These are suggested in a couple of cases brought by citizens who could wait the time it takes to get a civil suit through the Federal courts.

One of the first of these stemmed from cuts suffered by Mrs. Adeline Huslander of Elmira, New York, in 1961. Glass from a window broken by a sonic boom was the cause, and she sought what the law calls relief in Federal court. She ran into an obstacle in the statute allowing citizens to sue the government. Congress provided that if the damage was done by a Federal agency while carrying out its proper function—that is, if the claim is "based upon exercise or performance or the failure to exercise or perform a discretionary function or duty"—the citizen has no redress. Before the Huslander case got to trial, the government presented an affidavit from General Curtis LeMay, then Chief of Staff, to the effect that the planes that caused the boom had to fly over populated areas at supersonic speeds to learn how to meet an enemy at those speeds. The General did not mention that the same training could be given anywhere else, and Judge John O. Henderson dismissed Mrs. Huslander's suit.

The government did not offer this defense when Mrs. Arlene Naher of St. Paul, Minnesota, tried to recover $10,000 for damages that, she said, a series of sonic booms in 1962 did to an apartment building she owned. The Air Force had conducted an exercise of forty-one flights in two days at about twice the speed of sound along an air corridor that passed over the Naher building. Tenants testified to cracked plaster and broken windows on those days, and several months later, floors under the radiators settled, oak pillars cracked, doors sagged, and drainpipes broke—all because of weakening from the sonic boom, according to the complaint.

At the trial in 1967, government experts testified that sonic booms could not have done any of the damage. They asserted that the booms would not even have broken glass. They admitted, however, that a boom might cause an open window to slam down, but they insisted that it was the slam, not the boom, that did the damage. Judge Earl R. Larson, commenting that this might be valid scientifically but not legally, gave Mrs. Naher a little of what she asked. He did not think the evidence proved conclusively that the sonic booms had caused the structural damage to her 65-year-old building. He awarded her $750 for the glass and plaster. The delay of nearly five years between the destruction complained of and the court decision is not at all uncommon in Federal civil suits.

Airliners traveling at supersonic speeds may leave less doubt as to the destruction of which they are capable. The force of a sonic boom increases with the size of the object causing it. The crack of a whip is a small sonic boom, made as the lash that has been traveling faster than sound is brought to a halt. A military plane is smaller than any likely passenger transport, much smaller than experimental models already flown. Furthermore, the passenger planes will be faster, and that also increases the boom's force. Air Force exercises have been conducted usually at the speed of the one Mrs. Naher complained about, or less. The supersonic civilian jobs will fly at three times the speed of sound or more. One mitigating factor is that they will fly higher—about 60,000 feet as against the 30,000 to 50,000 of Air Force planes. The higher the object at the time the boom is created, the less the force. But on balance, the coming sonic booms can be expected to be much more destructive potentially than anything yet experienced.

By now many standard insurance policies contain a clause covering sonic-boom damage, and others specifically exclude it. Future battles will be between the insurance company representing the injured and another that has written the airline's liability policy. In these circumstances, one would expect settlements out of court in the vast majority of cases, but based on rules developed by the insurers and the regulating agencies.

When supersonic transports are common enough to raise the noise-pollution issue in earnest, state variations such as those of explosion law may complicate civilian operations. One simple regulation, already proposed in the New York Legislature, is to bar from the commonwealth's airports any plane guilty of noise above a certain level. The suggested maximum to be allowed is well below the din of experimental supersonic airliners now flown. Law of this kind, if put into effect, would force the technologists to eliminate objectionable features. Noise reduction is almost never impossible in any man-made machine. It simply costs money. The evolution of acceptable planes to fly at 2,000 miles an hour or so may well be brought about through the unique genius of our Federal system.

12 | On Solid Ground

One day in the spring of 1955 a developer, red-faced with anger, rose from a chair in the offices of Dr. William A. Holla, Commissioner of Health for Westchester County, New York's biggest bedroom suburb, and shouted:

"The banks won't let you do this to me!"

"You're mistaken," Dr. Holla replied, "the banks won't let you do this to the county."

The developer's "this" was the Health Department's refusal to give him occupancy permits for 45 new houses he had built and sold. He had long since spent the down payments and needed the balance to meet his loans. Dr. Holla's "this" was the stripping of topsoil from the entire development despite three departmental warnings. In the absence of topsoil, the septic tanks of the 45 houses would not handle the wastes of a modern household, and the development was too remote to be linked to a sewer line. Inspectors had explained to the developer before he broke ground that the department's standard required soil of sufficient quality to support a lawn. The warning was repeated during later inspections. The builder had merely sneered. It was his land, he said, and he could get $3 a load for thousands of loads of earth; let the purchasers of the houses get their own.

The man's understanding of the law (and of the banks) was faulty, a lapse for which he paid with bankruptcy when he was forced to replace the topsoil at about double the price he had received for it. Ten years earlier, he might have done as he pleased, and in plenty of jurisdictions, he still can. But more and more frequently, Law is reaching out to protect the land as well as the profits of those who own it. This stretching of the long arm of the Law is valid under the police power, as the rector and trustees of Trinity Church learned in 1895 (and as told in Chapter 1). As long as it seemed that our land was limitless and the soil endlessly self-renewing, its desecration by individuals or industry was deplored but still legal.

Industrial processes first roused Law to restrain the spoilers. In the earlier days, Law acted only after the fact, when someone could prove he had been damaged in some material sense. As early as 1904, for example, a Tennessee court ordered the Ducktown Sulphur, Copper & Iron Company to pay nearby landowners about $1,000 apiece because sulphurous fumes from the company's reduction facility killed trees and ruined the soil. The court, however, refused to enjoin the company or consider the plight of other landowners who were not parties to the suit. Shortly thereafter the company dropped the "Sulphur" from its title. It continued to smelt ore that was about 20 percent sulphur, and it introduced no devices to reduce the amount of the stuff that escaped in the smoke.

Ducktown is situated close to the corner where Tennessee meets North Carolina on the east and Georgia on the south. The prevailing winds carried the fumes of the plant, and of another that was even nearer the border, across into Georgia. In October 1905 *Georgia v. Tennessee Copper Company and Ducktown Sulphur & Iron Company* began a nine-year progress through the Federal courts. To begin with, the District Court in a ruling confirmed by the Supreme Court in 1907, gave the companies "a reasonable time" to reduce the proportion of sulphur in the smoke to an amount that would not kill plants in Georgia, about a mile from the Tennessee Copper facility and two and a half from Ducktown. Failing such a re- duction, the court would consider an injunction to prevent the furnaces from operating at all. Both companies installed purify- ing devices and cut the sulphur dioxide emitted about in half. This was still so destructive—averaging 35 tons a day from Ducktown alone, which was the smaller of the two smelters— that Georgia went back to court in 1913. A year later the Su- preme Court confirmed what seems now a rather mild judg- ment. It permitted emission of 20 tons of sulphur dioxide a day from April 10 to October 1, and 40 tons a day at other times. Yet in its time, the decision was considered so severe that Jus- tice Charles Evans Hughes protested: "I do not think that the evidence justifies the decree limiting production as stated." Joining in this dissent were Justice Holmes and Chief Justice Edward D. White, who, like Holmes, had fought in the Civil War but on the Confederate side. Thanks to the progress of Science in the next fifty years, it is doubtful that any members of the present Supreme Court would consider the old sulphur emissions justified.

Science on the one hand confirmed the harm that massive doses of sulphur dioxide can do to the land but also brought forth new processes and new amenities of life that were just as hard on the soil. The developer who stamped out of Dr. Holla's office in 1955 was only giving his customers the conveniences most Americans take for granted—plenty of heat and hot water, washing machines, dishwashers, kitchen garbage grind- ers, extra bathrooms. These and the packaging of food, cloth- ing and other articles in increasingly durable containers cre- ated problems of waste disposal that virtually forced Law to intervene, as Dr. Holla had been authorized to do. Urban and suburban communities especially were in danger of being buried, drowned or smothered in their wastes. Houses without proper defenses, either a septic tank or a link to a good sewer system, are a menace to health. The spread of regulations to require one or the other is hardly questioned in the courts on constitutional grounds anymore. Now health authorities go to law to enforce their standards. One of the most drastic court rulings of its kind turned what had been planned as a New Jersey suburban community of 580 middle-class homes into a premature ghost town.

In August 1966, 140 of the houses had been built and others were in various stages of construction. Then a State Superior Judge, James Rosen, signed an order at the request of the New Jersey Department of Environmental Protection, forbidding any new sewers to be linked to the system that served Jersey City and nine communities in the northern part of Morris County. The new development, called Fleetwood Homes by the developer, Osias Construction Company, had planned to tie into the system, and its lawyers argued insistently that newcomers have rights. About 100,000 people in the nine communities were already using the system in addition to Jersey City, which had built the treatment plant more than forty years before to protect its nearby water reservoir. By 1966, the flow from all the sewers emptying into the plant was as much as three times its capacity on some days. The overflow went on down the Rockaway River to pollute other towns downstream. Residents half a mile from the overworked treatment plant said that its vapors were strong enough to peel the paint from their houses.

Under these circumstances, Judge Rosen held that the loss to Osias—and to merchants and others who joined the company's plea to tell how much business the decision would cost them—was unfortunate but necessary. The people already on the land were entitled to protection, and the homeseekers who were denied a place on the already overburdened soil were being protected too. They were being barred from homes that might well become health hazards. Plans for larger and better treatment plants were drafted; but actual construction takes time, and nearly six years after Judge Rosen's ruling, Fleetwood Homes remained unoccupied.

This ghost town is a monument to Law's increasing concern that the ground we live on should be saved from the people who live on it. But just as some people use technology in their own interest only under compulsion—running water, proper sanitary disposal, fireproof stairs in certain buildings, and so on—others need Law's help in avoiding the excesses of technology. Scientists are as aware of this as lawyers. In December 1970, Bentley Glass remarked in his presidential address to the American Association for the Advancement of Science:

"Indeed, so awesome is already the accelerating rate of our scientific and technical advance that simple extrapolation of the exponential curves shows unmistakably that we have at most a generation or two before progress must cease, whether because the world's population becomes insufferably dense, or because we exhaust the possible sources of physical energy, or because, most likely of all, we pollute our environment to toxic, irremediable limits."

That last could hardly fail to happen in the present stage of technology if the dream of getting all mankind the machines that make possible the American way of life were to come true. We may be able, in Dr. Glass's words, "to flag the runaway express" if Law obliges Science to turn its full attention from research and technology for their own sakes to finding means to preserve the land.

A specific example of what this might entail is the almost frantic search for some method of disposing of the solid wastes accumulating at an ever-increasing rate in this country. They not only grow bulkier but become less degradable with every new technical "advance." In a city like New York, this is more than two tons a year for every man, woman and child, much of it building up from the so-called improvements in packaging, communications, construction, manufacturing, and getting rid of gaseous and liquid wastes.

The nonreturnable bottle, the aluminum can, and the fancy paper or plastic container account for more than half of all the debris that has to be hauled away—paper alone is nearly half that total when one adds newspapers and magazines to the packaging materials. Rubble from construction, old automobiles, crates, tools, clothes—thousands of products once salvaged or repaired—are thrown on the trash heap. Derelict cars alone, not worth selling to the car cemetery for scrap, pose a serious problem in big cities as their owners simply abandon them on the streets. Industrial processes discard valuable chemicals and metals because it is cheaper to buy fresh supplies than to reclaim wasted ones. Improved incineration and sewage treatment plants produce tons of solid sludge that used to go off to pollute air and water.

To reverse or control at least some of these trends before we run completely out of places to put the mountains of refuse is partly up to Law. Many law-making bodies from village boards to Congress are pondering ways to prevent much of the debris from happening at all or enforcing stricter methods of disposal. One method is to replace old-fashioned dumps with sanitary landfill. But convenient landfill sites are getting scarce. New York City is now completing its last one on Staten Island after making such good use of its opportunities that nearly 10 percent of its 365 square miles is land made from trash. Now the available new sites require expensive bulwarks or hauling over great distances.

New York and other cities have dumped so much waste into the Atlantic that fisheries and beaches have been polluted all down the Atlantic coast. In 1970, the Federal government closed 120 square miles of ocean to commercial fishing because of the health hazard. A Senate Sub-committee on Air and Water Pollution was considering a bill to require that all dumping in the ocean be beyond the continental shelf. In some areas, little is left to save. Off New York and New Jersey, the commercial catch had dropped from 673,000,000 pounds in 1962 to 133,000,000 in 1969. Oysters, once taken to the tune of more than 30,000,000 pounds a year, were down to little more than 1,000,000.

An example of the effect of outraged public opinion, whether well-informed or not, followed the government's sinking of an old hulk loaded with obsolete nerve gas in international waters off the coast of Florida in the summer of 1970. Old ammunition of all kinds had been dumped in the ocean routinely for a hundred years, but this time the antipollution outcry became so fierce that in 1971 the Defense Department announced abandonment of the practice for all weapons.

Laws to force the American people to reuse or recycle many materials they now throw away are being considered seriously. Some propose taxation; others rely on subsidy. Proponents of this legislation hope to bring back the returnable bottle, and the can and wastepaper salvage drives already begun by volunteer initiative of both private groups and industry. During periods when men and machines were scarce, as during the Korean War, up to 75 percent of the paper was collected and put back into the mills. Now it is argued that the cost of getting rid of old paper is more than the extra cost of putting it back into the manufacturing process.

Similarly, Law could make profitable the reclaiming of metals now junked. It has been pointed out that no one throws out old gold. The price of iron and other scrap would not have to be that high to make salvage attractive. Or Law could set such severe penalties for waste that the same result would be obtained. A Resource Recovery Act of 1970 fell far short of that but did authorize the government to undertake studies of the problem. The legislative device is simple enough. Companies that cut down trees to make paper already get a depletion allowance on their Federal taxes. Freight rates, set by a Federal agency, are higher for scrap than for new metal. By merely reversing the impact of these regulations, Congress could create a powerful incentive to favor conservation over waste. The depletion allowances not only could be ended but a tax could be levied on new cuttings so that using up resources would be more expensive. Rates on scrap could be lowered and those on virgin ore or metal raised. Already legislation has been passed to finance experiments in such improved techniques as persuading housewives to separate their salvageable paper, glass, and metal from garbage, and then compact the garbage for feeding pigs—a practical disposal method once more widespread than it is now. Meanwhile, laws are proposed to tax everything sold at a rate of 1 percent of its retail price to amass a fund to pay municipalities for getting rid of it when it is discarded.

Legal devices are being sought to induce technicians to turn their attention to reducing the amount of refuse and garbage that is generated in the first place. The container problem —bottles and cans and plastic, which are all virtually indestructible by ordinary disposal methods—could be solved if someone came up with packaging for food and drink as efficient as the ice cream cone. You eat it after you have emptied it. All the scientists need do is find a tasty, edible substance that would be somewhat tougher than a cone. Perhaps it could be dissolved in water to make soup or be baked or just served with cheese like a cracker.

Another disposal method more nearly within the limits of current scientific knowledge is the transmutation of garbage into useful items. The process would be to break down the undesirable waste into its atoms through nuclear fission and then rebuild those atoms into any material that is needed.

Law also is being tested to determine whether land that is being destroyed either economically or aesthetically can be saved for the public. The demand for power, for example, has encouraged strip-mining of coal, and in the absence of any legislation to prevent it, this turns what had been pleasant woods or fields into huge, lifeless scars that are not only hideous but will be unproductive for generations. One attack has been made in West Virginia, where coal is the largest industry. A bill passed by the 1971 legislature forbade any strip-mining for two years in counties where none has yet been done. Another measure to abolish it throughout the state failed but is sure to be brought up again. The prohibition covers 22 counties; 25 continue the practice as of this writing. Another proposed approach for Law is Federal regulation of all mining, strip or underground, as it affects the environment.

A somewhat different approach is a citizens' suit filed in U. S. District Court against the Tennessee Valley Authority, largest single producer of electricity and largest purchaser of coal in the country. The citizens, three conservation organizations, ask the court to abrogate the Authority's contract with the strip mines. The contracts contain clauses by which the owners undertake rehabilitation of the land, but the plaintiffs contend these measures are ineffective even if attempted. The complaint also accused TVA of ignoring a legal requirement to file statements with the President's Council on Environmental Quality describing the impact that its coal purchases would have on the environment. The case might make it through the courts by 1974 if both sides are stubborn.

Another area where Law is being asked to save the land from the products of technology is the vast extent of wilderness that is still publicly owned. Again citizens, whose standing to initiate such litigation has been greatly advanced, as indicated in earlier chapters, are protesting threats by proposed recreation or real estate projects. That they have made any progress at all, although falling short of victory, is a minor miracle of Law.

Typical of the recreational battlefields are a complex of dude ranch, skiing, and general outdoor fun in Montana, headed by Chet Huntley of broadcast fame, and a ski resort planned by Walt Disney Productions in the Sequoia National Park. Objections to both were that they would destroy irreplaceable wilderness that should be preserved. The Huntley scheme succeeded in placating objectors enough to proceed by exchanging land. The Disney program ran head on against the Sierra Club, which was one of the successful plaintiffs in the action to halt the Hudson River Expressway. The Club sued the Departments of Agriculture and Interior to prevent them from granting permission for Disney to build the resort in a remote section of the park known as Mineral King.

The basis of the suit was that the two departments, which shared supervision of the area, had not complied with all the legal requirements for a decision. Although the Sierra Club's standing in this case seems to be no different than it was when it joined in the Hudson River suit, the U. S. Court of Appeals in California disagreed with its counterpart in New York on what the law says. The judges dismissed the case, a ruling that probably will stand up only if the Supreme Court has a change of heart, since it had refused to review the New York case.

If the Court confirms the New York decision, it will reduce the impetus to adopt statutes such as the Michigan encouragement of citizen suits (mentioned in Chapter 8). Congress is often inclined to allow Supreme Court rules to govern a controversial situation. Pushing for an act to authorize litigation by private citizens may win votes from conservationists, but it may also lose the support of influential bureaucrats, important segments of industry, and well-heeled campaign contributors. Legislative reluctance to defend inarticulate and unorganized people in the face of such pressure is one of the best justifications for what critics of the judicial power in our system call "judge-made law." The protection of the soil may lead to a great deal more of it.

On the other hand, public pressure on administrators may induce these servants of the public to compete with judges as saviors of grass and trees, wilderness and park, and land generally fit to live on. This actually happened when the first scenes of a modern version of the Klondike gold rush were enacted after the discovery of vast untapped oil fields in northern Alaska, far beyond the reach of even the most powerful tankers. Federal officials stopped the Alaska oil rush dead in its tracks. They explained that they had to know what the effects on the land would be before they permitted the irreversible construction of a pipeline to get the oil to a port where tankers could pick it up.

The strike, hailed as arriving barely in the nick of time to keep the oceans of petroleum we consume flowing, led to speedy formation of a consortium of seven big companies to work leases obtained from the State of Alaska. Their Alyeska Pipeline Service Company quickly drafted plans for a line that would run 800 miles across the Alaskan interior from the North Slope, where the oil was discovered, almost straight south to the port of Valdez on the Gulf of Alaska.

By 1970, without waiting for the formalities of the Environment Policy Act (see Chapter 8) to be cleared through the proper government departments, Alyeska accumulated great piles of the necessary pipe, four feet in diameter, in Alaskan dumps, and masses of heavy earth-moving machinery. The company expected to spend a billion dollars to build the line and was eager to begin. But a Federal judge issued an injunction against any start on the project pending Interior Department compliance with the law. The Department is the agency that would issue the permit for a pipeline, and early in 1971 it announced a delay while the issues were studied. These are complicated by land claims of Eskimos and Indians.

When Interior finally issued its required statement, it conceded that with the line running through permanently frozen ground subject to frequent earth tremors for much of its route, leaks would be inevitable and the effect upon the wildlife and the soil itself unpredictable. The Environment Protection Agency, which is obliged to comment on departmental statements of this kind, thereupon counseled further delay until all environmental factors could be thrashed out, including an alternate route through Canada. Although this would be twice as long and more than twice as expensive, Canada probably will want to build it anyway, so at least only one wilderness would have to be damaged. Whatever the result in the vast unknown territory of Alaska, at least responsible government officials were asking technology for the facts before condemning a big piece of the earth to destruction by a technological giant.

| *Part Three*

LAW, SCIENCE, AND PEOPLE

13 | In the Beginning . . .

Law usually adjusts with dignity to the shocks administered to her by Science. Eventually, she works out reasonable modifications or regulations for the technological marvels that triggered the shocks. But when human reproduction is concerned, dignity and reason flee. The birth of a baby depends, so far anyway, upon sex, and Law has always been bewildered by her sister three-letter word. Now Science is busily revealing secrets of heredity and genetics that may revolutionize the reproductive process. Already it has shown us how to eliminate intercourse. Soon it will give us a choice between babies carried in the mother's womb in the old-fashioned way and babies propagated, as one professor of moral theology put it, "outside the tabernacle of the human body." What Law will make of it all is clouded by her sorry record in dealing with the knowledge and techniques Science has introduced to the field of reproduction in the past.

Artificial insemination is not one of Science's most recent additions to man's ability to master nature, but it exhibits Law in all her frustrations with anything that has to do with sex. Animal breeders practiced artificial insemination for centuries, maybe as early as 300 B.C., certainly since the 1300's when Arabs found it a good way to improve the strain of their horses.

This occasioned no public denunciation by either Law or outraged puritans, for both always view the sexual behavior of animals as somehow cleaner or less distasteful than that of humans. Dr. John Hunter, one of Scotland's great gifts to medicine on many counts, successfully fertilized a woman with her husband's semen in 1785. Quite a few cases followed during the next century, and about a third of all the quarter of a million or so "test-tube babies" estimated to be alive in the United States today were produced from the husband's sperm. In 1890, Dr. Robert L. Dickinson, one of the finest gynecologists America ever had, and a pioneer in promoting maternal health, birth control, and legalized abortion, undertook donor insemination. He lived for sixty years after that, and encouraged others to follow his lead. By the time he died, perhaps as many as five thousand babies were being born in this way every year. No one has a very exact count because reporting the procedure is not mandatory, and the birth certificate usually carries the name of the mother's husband as father.

In virtually all instances, a physician performs the insemination with the semen of a donor he selects. This man is almost invariably unknown to the couple who will rear the child; doctors have learned to shy away from using some good friend or relative of the couple since emotional difficulties often crop up later. The practice has been greatly facilitated by the discovery that sperm can be kept frozen almost indefinitely and retain its virility. Yet artificial insemination is clearly legal in only one state, Oklahoma, and there only since 1967. Bills to legitimize it have been rejected, sometimes repeatedly, in New York, Virginia, Wisconsin, Minnesota, and Indiana. On the other hand the Ohio legislature killed a proposal to make donor insemination a crime on the part of both woman and physician. The only other statutory pronouncement on the subject seems to be a clause in New York City's Health Code of 1959 setting up sanitary safeguards, such as a medical examination for the donor. Lawyers disagree as to whether this implies that the practice is legal.

Only a few cases involving artificial insemination have reached the courts in the last fifty years, and in all but one an anonymous donor was employed. The exception is an English case in which a wife sought to have her marriage annulled on the ground of her husband's impotence. He countered by reporting that she had borne a child after being artificially inseminated with his semen. The court granted the annulment.

Issues at stake in other lawsuits have been the child's legitimacy, the obligation of the mother's husband to support the child, rights of visitation, adultery, and perhaps forgery. A great many additional questions could be asked: the donor's responsibility, the right of a child to sue his mother's husband (he can't sue his own father while a minor), the child's claim to the donor's estate, the physician's liability, the possibility of criminal prosecution. One English doctor has been jailed for listing the husband of an artificially impregnated woman as the father of her child. The technical forgery issue has not yet been raised in the courts of this country, or most of the other legal questions either, since the usual litigants here are couples whose marriages broke up after the wife had a baby by donor insemination.

One might suppose that since Law demands very convincing evidence before branding anyone a bastard, and most states no longer enter the fact on birth certificates, the issue would be excluded from artificial insemination. But the rancor that partners to a broken marriage can engender and the ambivalent attitude of Law in matters sexual are immune to the pleadings of mere common sense.

The judicial pronouncements in the whole field of artificial insemination have been contradictory, and until 1968 were binding on no other court than the one trying the particular case. Furthermore, some of the opinions most frequently cited in the legal literature are classified as "mere dicta." Quite often judges muse out loud about what they think are the proper solutions to problems suggested by the case before them but not exactly relevant to it and not really bearing on the decision. Yet these musings may acquire the force of law—at least until another court reverses them—and lawyers call the judicial ramblings "dicta."

Such was the first ruling on artificial insemination of which we have a record, *Orford v. Orford,* decided in Ontario in 1921 by Mr. Justice Orde. He made a deliberate detour from his remarks on the issue before him to declare that donor insemination constituted adultery on the part of the woman. His dictum has been accepted as sound law in as many United States courts as have repudiated it.

Mr. Justice Orde got his chance to express his views because Mrs. Orford sued her husband, who had left her, for support. He refused to pay; he said she had committed adultery after they parted, a fact he learned only when she became pregnant. She retorted that her pregnancy resulted from artificial insemination, and her lawyer argued that so utterly impersonal a practice could not be adulterous. The judge threw out Mrs. Orford's case because he believed her baby was the result of a normal fleshly relationship, but he was so shocked by what he considered her lawyer's perverse argument about the innocence of donor insemination that he characterized it forcefully:

"A monstrous conclusion surely! If such a thing has never before been declared adultery, then on the grounds of public policy, the Court should now declare it so."

Justice Orde went on to say that the real legal objection to adultery is that it risks introducing an alien strain into the blood lines of the woman's husband. A married man who has intercourse with a single woman is guilty because this constitutes "the voluntary surrender to another person of the reproductive powers or faculties of the guilty person." In his theory of the law, a venerable one, the mere sexual act is only moral turpitude; it is the danger of presenting the husband with a spurious heir that makes it a crime. Donor insemination is no less adultery than if the husband condoned his wife's taking a lover, according to this line of reasoning.

In the United States cases, the husband has nearly always consented. The language of our judges has been a little more restrained than that of Justice Orde, but about half of them agreed with him. In Great Britain, an English court granted a divorce on the ground that the wife committed adultery by being impregnated with a donor's semen, but a Scottish court refused a divorce after almost identical testimony, saying donor insemination is not adultery. In a case discreetly reported in 1949 as *L. v. L.*, another British tribunal held that artificial insemination with the husband's semen is an abnormal sexual act and therefore the child is illegitimate. French jurisprudence escapes the dilemma by holding the practice is against natural law and therefore forbidden.

The earliest United States decisions seemed to allow the Orde dictum no foothold in this country. In the very first, *Hoch v. Hoch* (1945), a Chicago Circuit Court refused the husband a divorce on grounds of adultery, the act complained of being donor insemination to which he had consented. This was an oral opinion, but it appears that the judge considered penetration by the male organ essential to adultery. Three years later *Strnad v. Strnad* came before a state court in New York City because Mrs. Strnad wanted to cancel her former husband's privilege of visiting their child, granted when they obtained a divorce. She pointed out that the child was the product of donor insemination and therefore not Strnad's legitimate offspring. The judge refused to label the child a bastard, asserting he was "potentially adopted or semi-adopted" with the same status as a child born out of wedlock, but later "legitimized by the marriage of the interested parties." Clearly artificial insemination with the husband's consent was not adultery in this court.

These two decisions may seem reasonable, but they were soon contradicted. In 1954, a Mrs. Doornbos sued for divorce in Chicago. She had had a son by donor insemination and asked the court to rule that the child was legitimate and that Doornbos should have no visiting rights. The judge did refuse to allow visiting rights but only because he said the child was illegitimate, adding:

"Artificial insemination by donor, with or without the consent of the husband, is contrary to public policy and good morals, and constitutes adultery on the part of the wife."

A somewhat similar lower court finding on legitimacy was reached by another New York state court in *Gursky v. Gursky* (1963). This time the husband wanted the child of donor insemination, to which he had consented, declared illegitimate so he would be relieved of its support. He also sought an annulment of his marriage. The judge rejected the Strnad doctrine. He explained that under the common law any child "born out of wedlock" is illegitimate and that the Family Court Act specifically defined this phrase as "a child begotten and born out of lawful matrimony." As for the adoption rationalization, the judge pointed out that children can be adopted in New York only under the Domestic Relations Law, which says nothing about donor insemination. Gursky lost his case anyway. The child's illegitimacy did not relieve him of the obligations that he assumed when he gave his consent to his wife's impregnation, the court explaining that this was an implied contract to support the child.

None of these or any other similar cases ever went to a higher court until 1968, and then the reasons for *People v. Sorenson* differed from those others, as the title suggests. The Sorenson divorce decree, issued in 1964, four years after the wife bore a son by donor insemination with her husband's consent, gave her custody and stipulated that she would not ask Sorenson for support. Two years later, she fell ill and applied for welfare, whereupon the district attorney took Sorenson into municipal court under a California statute that reads: "A father of either a legitimate or illegitimate minor child who wilfully omits without lawful excuse to furnish necessary . . . care for his child is guilty of a misdemeanor." Sorenson said this did not apply to him since he was not the boy's father, and anyway Mrs. Sorenson had waived support. The municipal magistrate was not impressed, and an appeal was taken to the California Court of Appeals. Here the judges unanimously rejected the waiver claim, saying that Mrs. Sorenson was not entitled to sign away her child's right to be supported. As to the disclaimer of paternity, the unanimous opinion written by Justice Mc-Comb noted that the boy's birth certificate carried Mr. Sorenson's name as father, and continued:

"One who consents to the production of a child cannot create a temporary relation to be assumed and disclaimed at will. It is less crucial to determine the status of the child than the status of the defendant as his father. Categorizing the child as either legitimate or illegitimate does not resolve the legal consequences flowing from the defendant's participation in the child's existence . . . no valid public purpose is served by stigmatizing an artificially conceived child as illegitimate."

The ruling also referred approvingly to Law's strong presumption of legitimacy and found that in this instance the presumption had not been overcome. Then Justice McComb went out of his way to provide some dicta of his own on the subject of donor insemination as adultery, writing:

"Since the doctor may be a woman, or the husband himself may administer the insemination by a syringe, this is patently absurd; to consider it an act of adultery with the donor who at the time of insemination may be a thousand miles away or may even be dead is equally absurd."

Law's tergiversations on this subject may be condoned because few of the potentially difficult artificial insemination questions have arisen. But if we adopt the proposals of eminent scientists to establish sperm banks, whether to improve the race or simply to extend the potential posterity of the banks' founders, Law may have to look more closely at the implications. And if the genetic engineers discover that they can bypass nature's clumsy reproductive methods altogether, Law's task will be profoundly difficult.

The most distinguished proponent of sperm banks was the Nobel Prize winner, Hermann J. Muller. He suggested they be established first for every young man who is in the armed forces or is exposed to more than average radiation. Those who are killed or become impotent or are likely to produce deformed offspring because of the radiation would have healthy sperm available to fertilize their wives. Dr. Muller also thought banks should be established with the sperm of selected individuals as a means of improving as well as preserving the population.

Law's problems are obvious. What sort of Federal Reserve System would we need to regulate the banks? Can the founder control access to it entirely? Would single women be eligible for withdrawals? Would married women need the written consent of their husbands? What happens to a trust fund that is being held for distribution until the testator's youngest grandchild reaches twenty-one if one of the sons sets up a sperm bank? (Professor Barton W. Leach of the Harvard Law School postulated this last dilemma in an article he called "The Case of the Fertile Decedent." He suggested that the estate never would go to any of the intended heirs because the sperm bank would hold open the possibility of another grandchild until all of them were dead.)

Confusing? Perhaps, yet the legal future of artificial insemination is predictably simple compared to that of the real test-tube baby, one manufactured in the laboratory from synthetic genes and nurtured in an incubator. A Mr. Justice Orde would doubtless rule that the product is not a person at all and therefore entitled to none of the rights and protections of a human being. Legislatures and courts will have to settle on who is permitted to create a baby, who has the obligation to support it, what are the duties and privileges of the resulting individual. The determination of the types to be created could hardly be left to the whims and fancies of any couple who want to take the trouble to make a baby. That is what happens now, and one can only guess at how much misery has followed. It would be much worse when the couple could get the baby they want, not have to take what they get from the cumbersome natural system.

Struggles over regulating the process by legislation, and litigation to determine the legislation's meaning will be awesomely fierce. Simplest of all will be those domestic lawsuits, the *Doe v. Doe* of the future, when both want to order a star but hers is to be in the movies and his on the football field. Will the Solomon who hears the case decree that they have twins? Much more difficult will be decisions as to what genes should be outlawed and which encouraged. Should procreation by a man and woman as we know it be permitted in any circumstances? How many scientists should be produced in proportion to laboratory technicians or historians or truck drivers? Will the state itself have to produce and rear the hewers of wood and drawers of water whom no parent orders?

Along the way, Law may gain some useful experience with lesser but still highly controversial scientific advances. It may become possible to determine precisely whether any couple will produce offspring with undesirable traits or handicaps and whether these have appeared in the fetus. Will Law seek to identify the desirable and set up machinery to eliminate the undesirable? And what machinery? Routine abortion? Inform the parents and leave it to them? Trust the physician? Do nothing and hope Science will discover ways to overcome the undesirable traits before it is too late?

Much of the genetic study going on is directed toward eliminating congenital diseases and malformations. When this progresses to the point of reliable prediction, Law may well require all couples to be examined for freedom from dangerous genes as they now must undergo blood tests to assure freedom from venereal disease. They may even be required to show that their offspring will be suitable for life in an increasingly complex society.

The thought is rather horrendous, but the result might just be a way out of the danger that the Harvard biologist, George Wald, described in the *Bulletin of Atomic Scientists* in 1969. He pointed out that the dinosaur was impressively muscled and armored but had a very small brain in proportion. The vast power with small intelligence to guide it led to extinction while mammals and eventually man supplanted the dinosaur as the dominant earth creature. Man, according to Wald, has a beautiful balance of brain and brawn, the largest brain in proportion to brawn in the animal kingdom. But, he added, put man in a car and all of a sudden you have somewhat the proportion of brain to power and armor that destroyed the dinosaur. Give him bombers, rockets, intercontinental missiles and all the astronomically magnified brawn of our military hardware and the dinosaur becomes a comparatively better balanced beast. Law may yet have to guide Science if we are not to let genetics carry that example through to its logical conclusion.

14 | Law

When It's Life or Death

In a country whose wise men are not sure when life has either
begun or ended, Law finds herself in recurring difficulties. Up
to now, she has tended to accept the theologians' definitions of
life and the physicians' of death. Since neither all the clerics nor
all the doctors agree on either, Law's own expositions are not
always clear. But Science's medical, surgical, and biochemical
progress is forcing Law toward a position of her own, not only
when life and death need to be defined but also on social controls over such procedures as organ transplants, sterilization,
genetic engineering, euthanasia, and the use of scarce medical
facilities and personnel. The difficulties in reaching that position were well stated in 1968 by Dunkers and Dukeminier in
Medical Advances and Law:

"Scientific technology and medical research have ushered
us precipitately into a civilization for which our legal institu-
tions are not prepared. . . . But medical technology is power,
and the supervision of power is, in our civilization, the first
function of law. If history is a guide, many problems incubated
in hospitals will mature in the courts."

Two years later, in 1970, a problem, incubated by Science,
did reach the courts, although it could hardly be said to have
matured there. It involved a Kentucky family with two grown

sons. The elder could probably be saved for a long and useful life if one of his brother's kidneys was transplanted into his body. The family and their medical advisers were not permitted to decide for themselves if the operation should be performed. That was left to Law; and in *Strunk v. Strunk*, Law gave her answer.

Tommy Strunk, married, 28 years old, and going to college part-time while working, was found to have a terminal kidney ailment, reversible in the present state of medical knowledge only by a kidney transplant. His parents and other relatives were examined as potential donors. The process is not dangerous, since we function just about as well with one kidney as two, but a very careful match is necessary. None of the family was suitable medically except brother Jerry, 27, who was described by the surgeons as a perfect donor. The legal trouble was that Jerry had been for years in a state institution for the feebleminded. With an IQ of 35 and a mental age of 6, he was not fit to decide for himself whether or not to give a kidney. Nor, in the eyes of most courts, are parents fully competent to make such decisions for their children. The temptation to favor a Tommy over a Jerry is considered more than parents should be asked to meet. So Mrs. Strunk, who had been appointed years before to look after Jerry's interests, petitioned the county court to authorize the transplant operation.

At the hearing, a guardian assigned to represent Jerry for the occasion questioned whether a kidney donation was in the young man's best interests. The court ruled that it was, partly because Jerry "would be jeopardized more severely by the loss of his brother [testimony had shown that Tommy was his closest tie to the family] than by the removal of a kidney." The guardian appealed, lost in the state court and appealed again to the Kentucky Court of Appeals. Here the decision was close, but by four to three the transplant was authorized.

To the minority, the operation smacked of Nazi experiments with living bodies. They were not impressed by evidence that minors, who need parental consent for almost any operation, had been allowed to donate kidneys. The three judges pointed out that all these youngsters were in their teens, quite old enough to know what they were doing. The majority did not think that Jerry should be deprived of the chance to do a good deed just because he was a mental six-year-old. They referred to medical testimony that it would be good for him to play such a helpful role in the family, and at no greater risk than men assume in driving a car sixteen miles a day. The dissenters were not convinced by the experts or by the evidence that indicated Jerry would suffer severe shock if Tommy died.

Neither side was influenced by the wishes of Mrs. Strunk. In considering a child's welfare, Law looks askance at parents as the fount of all wisdom. In many situations, Law prefers the state as protector of the young. The Supreme Court took this position in 1944 in *Prince v. Massachusetts:*

"The State has a wide range of power for limiting parental freedom and authority in things affecting the child's welfare. Parents may be free to become martyrs themselves. But it does not follow that they are free, in identical circumstances, to make martyrs of their children before they have reached the age of full and legal discretion when they can make the choice for themselves."

One must make allowances for such judicial exuberance. The "martyrdom" of which this decision speaks—a five-to-four ruling at that—was Mrs. Sara Prince's consent to let her nine-year-old niece join her in distributing Jehovah Witness tracts on a Boston street in violation of the state's child-labor laws. Testimony showed that the child had begged to do it. She herself testified that she knew it was her religious duty because it was God's desire, and if she failed by not being permitted to sell leaflets, she faced "everlasting destruction at Armageddon." While four justices declared the act neither martyrdom nor child labor but a perfectly reasonable if nonconformist exercise of religion, the majority rule is often cited to show the limits of a parent's desires or authority in bringing up a child.

It also explains the limits of a parent's right to give away a child's kidney. But the Strunk majority needed, or at least wanted, an old foundation on which to rest its judgment that the gift could be made. They found it in an English case of 1816, *Ex parte Whitebread*. Whitebread, like Jerry Strunk, was an institutionalized incompetent. He had a large estate and poor brothers and sisters. Could his guardian use some of his money to support them? The Lord Chancellor replied that it would be quite proper since it was the sort of generosity normal people enjoy dispensing, and he added:

"The Court will not refuse to do for the benefit of the Lunatic that which it is probable the Lunatic would have done."

The Kentucky court's analogy between money and an organ of the body was clearer in 1816 than today. For Law has drawn the proprietary distinction since then, largely during this century. When Judge Cardozo gave a series of famous lectures on "The Growth of the Law" at the Yale Law School in 1923, he noted that in this very year the second highest court in New York State had confirmed a legal doctrine at least three hundred years old, for Sir Edward Coke had expressed it as meaning that a man has a property right in the body of his wife, although she has none in the body of her husband.

The New York court had been hearing the story of a fairly common domestic tragedy. Jennie Oppenheim, separated from her husband in 1913 after 24 years of marriage, had never reconciled herself to his finding solace with another woman. She learned that this woman was Martha Kridel, a widow, with whom Oppenheim began living in 1917. In January 1919, witnesses for Mrs. Oppenheim found them in an apartment "under such circumstances as to leave no doubt that they had committed adultery." The pair freely confessed that. But Mrs. Oppenheim was not looking for divorce evidence. She wanted revenge. She sued Mrs. Kridel for alienation of her husband's affections, although one would suspect from her story that she had lost them before he ever met the widow. The first judge who heard the case told her she should sue on grounds of "criminal conversation," a legal euphemism of the day meaning that the husband was giving to another the sexual faculties he owed exclusively to his wife. This judge instructed that jury that they could consider the loss of affections only as a factor in assessing damages, along with Mrs. Oppenheim's mental anguish and her disgrace as a rejected wife.

The Appellate Division, the next court up the ladder, reversed the jury's award. These judges, at least a majority of them, held to the old doctrine of property rights in a spouse's body. Mrs. Oppenheim had none and therefore could have no claim as a result of "criminal conversation," although her husband would have had a perfect case if their situations were reversed. Judge Cardozo's court, the state's highest, overturned this ruling. Commenting on the Coke theory of conjugal rights, Cardozo said in his Yale lecture:

"We did not ignore these precedents, but we held them inconclusive," a judicially polite way in which courts often overrule the wisdom of the past. "Decisions founded upon the assumption of a bygone inequality were unrelated to present-day realities, and ought not to be permitted to prescribe a rule of life."

The actual opinion of the court in *Oppenheim v. Kridel*, not written by Cardozo although he concurred, is quoted more often than his lecture by lawyers arguing for a reversal of past decisions. It includes this statement:

"The common law is not rigid and inflexible, a thing dead to all surrounding and changing conditions; it does expand with reason. The common law is not a compendium of mechanical rules, written in fixed and indelible characters, but a living organism which grows and moves in response to the larger and fuller development of the nation."

This concept draws Law slowly along the road toward a formula that takes advantage of new medical techniques while avoiding some of the obvious dangers. The need for such a balance has been clearly exposed by successful heart transplants. When one heart is available and two patients are equally suitable subjects for the operation, which one gets it? Who decides one is more suitable than the other? Granting that surgeons may be the best judges, can they equitably pursue this sort of practice without legal guidelines? Would they be called upon to defend their judgment in court? Are a man's organs his to leave after death? Above all, when is he dead?

The last two questions appear to be the only ones that have led to any considerable search for answers, and neither Law nor Science has sounded a very certain trumpet as yet. Until recently, Law comfortably accepted the rule that a man is dead when a physician says so. The question was purely academic unless the time of death was important, as in settling an estate or when it might be relevant in a murder trial. A frequently cited definition is from *Black's Law Dictionary*. The 1968 edition says this: "the cessation of life; the ceasing to exist; defined by physicians as the total stoppage of the circulation of the blood, and a cessation of the animal and vital functions consequent thereon, such as respiration, pulsation, etc."

The transplant surgeon's problem is that by the time all this has been definitely established, it may be too late to use the heart. So for his purpose, the concept of "cerebral death" has gained some favor. In its simplest terms, this was defined by a Harvard committee in 1968 as "irreversible coma." This lacks precision for both Law and Science. One of the proposals for elaborating on it suggests that death should be presumed after three conditions are met. First, the doctor finds no reflexes, no spontaneous breathing, no muscle activity. Second, the patient does not respond, even on an electroencephalogram, to noise or a pinch. Third, the same results are obtained after the lapse of at least 24 hours. Yet lawyers have argued that a surgeon who removes the heart from a patient after all these tests might be committing homicide. They point out that many doctors say a man is alive as long as a heartbeat and breathing can be detected, even if these are maintained artificially. Presumably if a surgeon were brought to trial under these circumstances, a jury of laymen would have to decide his fate. They would have the help and guidance of expert testimony (probably conflicting) and the judge's charge, but it seems doubtful that they would rely upon anything except their prejudices.

While nothing so spectacular has yet arisen, some physicians express doubts about the morality of actual practices. Donors have been declared dead one day, although the heart was not removed until the next. In one case, the body was taken to another state, apparently traveling as a living person, and while it may seem a quibble to object, lawsuits and criminal charges have sprung from less.

Both medical and legal authorities are timid in prognosticating when and how this difficulty will be resolved. New advances may disprove even the most reasonable theories. Until the 1940's, no physician would have hesitated to pronounce dead a patient who had suffered a cardiac arrest. Then a Dr. Claude Beck showed that the stopped heart could be started again; if it was done within four minutes, before the brain was damaged by lack of oxygenated blood, a complete recovery was possible. Another example: A few years ago anyone who raised a question about the ownership of a man's heart, or any other organ, would have been considered frivolous. While he lived, they were his. After his death, they belonged to the next of kin. Today, since many tissues and organs are valuable for research and for transplants, most states have laws that oblige the next of kin to honor their dead relative's donations of his organs, but the red tape may defeat a testator's purpose.

While Law struggles with issues raised by transplants from the living or those just dead, Science moves on toward establishment of banks of frozen or synthetic organs upon which anyone will be able to draw. Some visionaries suggest that Science will even permit the healthy to escape from their own time into the future. The notion that the whole man could be frozen and kept in storage to be thawed out at the date of his choice, when presumably earth will have become a better place to live, appeals to some. Whether Law would allow him to reclaim his estate or even his identity is a nice question. Would he have special privileges to adjust to the new conditions he finds before being committed to a mental institution? What property belongs to him if any? How old is he?

More frightening, and in the opinion of a few experimenters more imminent, are the issues foreshadowed by work already being done on the brain. If a transplant should ever become possible, Law might not easily determine who the living individual really is. Suppose an elderly brain is grafted inside the skull of a young man. The memories and knowledge presumably would be elderly, the physique youthful. Would Law take the position that the elderly gentleman had acquired a new body or that the young fellow got a new brain? Again questions of property arise. And to whom is the recovered man married—the wife he can identify or the wife who can identify him?

Biology also offers reason to suppose that we may one day be able to improve the intelligence of animals, even to the point of developing an ape with the mental capacity of a man. Would "it" become a person with full rights of citizenship? Would it remain the property of its owner? Would the human developer be prosecuted for loosing a monster on society? Would the compulsory education laws apply? Would it be permitted to acquire and bequeath property?

The puzzle of death is almost inseparable in Law from the puzzle of life. Is one more than just the absence of the other? The dilemma is clear in the case of a helpless human being for whom medical science as it exists here and now can see no hope of survival. Law does not require the physician to employ extraordinary measures such as respirators or continuous blood transfusions. But Law does not authorize the physician to withhold such measures either. As for the positive solution of euthanasia—a painless death when doctors agree agony or anaesthesia are the only alternatives—Law calls it murder.

Law gives no guidance to the administrators and medical chiefs of a hospital who know that the care required for a heart transplant could, if efficiently distributed, serve a dozen or more dangerously ill people who now get virtually no medical attention. One of the country's prestige hospitals, Massachusetts General in Boston, declined a few years ago to go in for such transplants for this reason. Although it had one of the best teams for this type of surgery, it decided the sacrifice of talent was too great. The doctors and nurses whose time this one patient would monopolize could minister to twenty just as needy or deserving.

Law's ambiguity in dealing with death, and medical efforts to avert it, is clarity itself when compared to her attitude toward life. Her definitions of this simple word have complicated generations of legal disputes over birth control, abortion, and sterilization. The first two were until recently forbidden to all women except as prescribed by a doctor. The third was not only permitted but in more than half the states could be imposed upon certain categories of the inhabitants.

Because Law had taken its cue on contraception and abortion from religious or moral precepts, these medical procedures were hedged about with all sorts of semiofficial obstacles. Slowly and partly these gave way to Science. Physicians were permitted to prescribe contraceptives, mostly by court decision but in a few states by statute, without elaborate formalities. Abortion rules were gradually relaxed. The first concession required the doctors to certify the operation was essential to save the mother's life. The most recent is New York's 1970 reform, permitting the woman and her doctor to make the decision on whatever grounds appear reasonable to them. Elsewhere, prohibitory laws have been eased. In 1969, the California Supreme Court upset the conviction of a physician who had referred a young woman to an unlicensed abortionist. The judges held that the statutory phrase "necessary to preserve her life" is too vague to be a proper guide to medical practices. It always put the doctor in jeopardy if he performed the operation but never if he did not. Noting that an abortion in the first three months is now less likely to be fatal than carrying a child to term, the court suggested Law had been changed by medical progress.

These shifts are interesting to trace, but judicial and legislative rulings on sterilization, far less enmeshed in emotional controversy than birth control and abortion, are more revealing of Law's trend in life or death. In practice, Law has never interfered in the sterilization under medical safeguards of either men or women who desired it. It is a simple, safe, virtually painless procedure for a man, and for a woman, too, if the operation is performed at the time she is delivered of a baby, which is when many mothers of several children request it. Sterilization becomes a serious legal issue when it is ordered by the state. So far in this country, the state has attempted it only for mental defectives and criminals. Law has not had to rule on the power of a legislature to extend the practice to other undesirables, or people the majority consider undesirable.

The Supreme Court took its first step toward clarifying the issue in 1927 when Justice Holmes wrote the opinion of the Court, one member dissenting, in *Buck v. Bell.* This was a test of a Virginia law permitting the sterilization of institutionalized incompetents who suffered from any hereditary form of insanity or imbecility. The statute stipulated that hearings and judicial review of the findings were to be mandatory, and a guardian for the intended victim was to be present at all stages.

This procedure had been followed in the case of Carrie Buck, a white girl, who in 1924 was an inmate in the Virginia State Colony of Epileptics and Feeble-Minded. She was 18, daughter of a feebleminded mother in the same institution, and

Carrie had given birth to a feebleminded child. At the request of Superintendent Bell of the Colony, a special board issued an order for an operation to cut the girl's Fallopian tubes. The Virginia courts had upheld the order, and the case came to the Supreme Court on a plea that Carrie's constitutional rights were being violated, notably the Fourteenth Amendment's guarantee against "deprivation of life, liberty, or property, without due process of law."

In his argument, Carrie's counsel invited the court to consider the danger opened up by sterilization laws, crying: "A reign of doctors will be inaugurated and in the name of science new classes will be added, even races be brought within the scope of such regulation." He then went back fifty years to one of the early tests of the Fourteenth to quote triumphantly from *Munn v. Illinois,* which had been decided in 1876:

"By the term 'life' as here used in the Fourteenth Amendment something more is meant than mere animal existence. The inhibition against its deprivation extends to all those limbs and faculties by which life is involved."

One assumes that Munn was about to be mutilated by the State of Illinois, but a reading of the case discloses a less dramatic though still important legal point. Munn was partner in a firm that operated a grain elevator in Chicago. All that Illinois asked of him was that he obtain a warehouse license and charge no more than the two cents a bushel that a state law fixed as the maximum for storing wheat. When he refused, Illinois fined him $100. Justice Stephen J. Field had uttered the colorful passage quoted by Carrie's lawyer in explaining that in his view the Fourteenth Amendment gave the same protection to property as it did to life and liberty. Therefore, a man could charge as much as he liked for the use of his own property, and did not need a state license to do it.

Although Carrie's lawyer did not say so, Justice Field had persuaded only one of his eight brethren. Chief Justice Morrison R. Waite had brushed aside the Field argument in 1876, saying the Fourteenth Amendment was not an issue. From far back in English common law and still in ours, the police power permitted the state to demand licenses of and to fix prices for businessmen who serve the public. He found it unnecessary to define either life or liberty for the purpose of reaching this decision.

The attempt to equate Carrie's Fallopian tubes with the grain business failed. The 1927 court, with one exception, preferred Virginia's reasoning that this case fell within the police power as reasonably as the authority to compel vaccination, even over religious objections, or to confine the insane to segregated quarters where they could not procreate. The opinion also noted that after her operation, Carrie could be allowed to live in her own home town, since she was capable of earning a living and was dangerous to no one. She would cease to be a charge on the state.

"We have seen more than once that the public welfare may call upon the best citizens for their lives," Justice Holmes wrote. "It would be strange if it could not call upon those who already sap the strength of the State for these lesser sacrifices, often not felt to be such by those concerned, in order to protect our being swamped with incompetence. Three generations of imbeciles are enough."

Science's ability to recognize hereditary feeblemindedness, at least in certain instances, was responsible for the Holmes decision. This became clear fifteen years later when his successors had to deal with another category of people declared ripe for sterilization by a state legislature. This time the appeal was against an Oklahoma statute that authorized the operation for habitual criminals. The Supreme Court did not overrule *Buck v. Bell* and made a point of saying so because "We are dealing here with . . . one of the basic civil rights of man." The facts were these:

In 1935, when Oklahoma adopted a statute authorizing sterilization of anyone convicted twice or more of "crimes amounting to felonies involving moral turpitude," J. T. Skinner was in prison for armed robbery. He had served a previous prison term for the same offense and in 1926 had been convicted of stealing chickens. In 1936, the state Attorney General brought proceedings under the new act to have Skinner sterilized. The law stipulated that the jury should hear no evidence as to the hereditary nature of Skinner's criminal tendencies. They were to consider, and the trial judge so charged them, only two points: Had he been twice convicted of a felony? Would the operation impair his health? The jurors answered yes to the first and no to the second, and the appeals started.

The state Supreme Court upheld the verdict, and on May 6, 1942, *Skinner v. Oklahoma* was argued before the U. S. Supreme Court. Within a month, the nine justices agreed that Oklahoma had exceeded its police powers, but they were not unanimous on their reasons for that opinion.

Justice Douglas, writing for the majority, said one feature of the Oklahoma statute was so discriminatory that the court did not need to consider any of the other objections to it. The flaw was a clause stating that embezzlers, violators of prohibitory laws, tax cheats, and political offenders were exempted from sterilization procedures. The legislators had not said that these crimes involved no moral turpitude, and Justice Douglas wrote that surely no basis existed for believing that embezzlers were eugenically different from chicken thieves, or tax cheats from other swindlers. He was afraid that if the Court upheld this sort of discrimination, the next such bit of legislation might justifiably confine sterilization to members of a certain race or nationality.

Chief Justice Harlan Fiske Stone concurred with the result but not the reasoning. He wrote that the Court must presume the legislature knew something science did not—that one class of criminals passes on its criminal tendencies more than another. He was willing to take the word of the Oklahoma statesmen for it, although he conceded that scientists would not. But,

he added, the Constitution demands that any individual sin-
gled out by this inspired legislative vision must have a chance
to show he is not in the proscribed category. Furthermore, in
the absence of any scientific evidence, the burden of proof is on
the state to prove that any particular group or individual is in
that category.

Justice Robert Jackson, in another concurring opinion,
agreed with both Douglas and Stone. He thought each of the
opinions should have included the other. He pointed out more
clearly than the others that what distinguished *Buck v. Bell*
from *Skinner v. Oklahoma* was the completeness of the hearing
in Virginia, the necessity for scientific findings, and the lack of
discrimination between groups of imbeciles.

All this suggests more questions than answers for Law.
What will the choice of life and death be in the future? Who
will make the decisions when Science is able to identify potential criminals and genetic carriers of imbecility or infirmity?
Who may have children? Who may receive a new heart or a
new brain? Who may be placed in cold storage to await better
times? Can individuals be trusted to choose each for himself?
Can the State? Law will have to weigh the risks against the
benefits in formulating her replies.

15 | Law
in the Alimentary Canal

Almost everything we swallow nowadays—food and drink,
pills and potions—has been refined if not created by Science in
the last generation. New ways of preserving and processing
food and the discovery of thousands of new drugs have revolutionized the kitchen and the sickroom. Law has been trying to
catch up with technology in these matters for nearly a century
in a struggle that began simply to keep us from being poisoned
and continues in the hope of assuring the full benefits that
modern techniques have promised us. Until the early 1900's, it
was no race; Law was nowhere. Since 1906, technology has felt
Law's hot breath on the back of its neck and sometimes actually gets collared. The recurring cry that consumers need protection from dangerous or misrepresented food and drugs is
still justified all too often, but the basic issue was settled more
than half a century ago after nearly thirty years of legislative in-
fighting.

In keeping with the genius of our Federal system, the earliest attempts to safeguard the public were undertaken by the
states. During the last half of the 19th century, the industrial
processing of food and the manufacture of drugs began to replace mother's preserving or canning and grandma's home-
grown remedies for anything that ailed the family. Packers and

canners were soon a major industry, selling their wares chiefly in the cities. Patent medicine fakers were at least as successful in rural as in urban areas. The profits were enormous and could be increased by adulteration. A quart of milk became three pints by adding water. Spoiled, rancid food was treated with formaldehyde to disguise the telltale aroma of decay and with sulfate of copper to improve its appearance. Mixing a few flavoring ingredients with alcohol and water or compounding pills from sugar and any cheap ingredients that struck the maker's fancy, the unscrupulous sold cure-alls by outdoing their rivals in extravagant claims. Herrick's Vegetable Pills, for example, were labeled as a cure (not merely a reliever) for dyspepsia, colic, sick headaches, constipation, diarrhea, worms, fever, ague, and indigestion.

When contractors delivered "embalmed beef" to the Army during the war with Spain, causing more casualties than enemy fire, the scandal was already an often-told tale. The public had been getting sick from processed food for years, and most of the states had enacted some sort of remedial legislation. Usually they demanded truth in labeling, some even going so far that a popular breakfast food, Grapenuts, would be outlawed unless it contained both grapes and nuts. Other statutes attempted to establish sanitary rules. Their most serious drawbacks were that they could not reach across state lines, and they provided little or no inspection.

As early as 1879, a congressional bill proposed Federal regulation of food in interstate commerce. By the time Theodore Roosevelt won his second term in the White House, about two hundred such measures had been quietly buried in either the House or Senate before they ever came to a vote. No one spoke against any of them. They were simply passed over in the press of other legislation. But public opinion was aroused by Upton Sinclair's portrayal of packing-plant horrors in *The Jungle,* and by the era's other talented muckrakers who wrote the most popular periodical literature of the day. People read in their favorite magazines and newspapers about widely sold nostrums for babies that were nothing but morphine, opium or laudanum—no one yet objected much to heroin, as it was then known chiefly as an excellent cough medicine. For those who were impressed by figures, the writers noted that the nation spent more on quack medicines than defense. Much of the information for these articles came from a Department of Agriculture chemist, Harvey W. Wiley, who had been crusading for Federal regulation since 1902. That year, he organized a group of testers who became known as "the poison squad" for their revelations about the preservatives and additives in processed American food.

Stimulated by all this, the President plunged into the controversy after Congress let still another bill die in 1905. Late that year, in his annual message, he demanded "a law . . . to regulate interstate commerce in misbranded and adulterated food, drink, and drugs." He kept the issue alive and sustained public pressure by his enthusiasm. Prodded by constituents and wary of the presidential patronage club, Congress passed the Pure Food and Drugs Act, signed on July 30, 1906. Roosevelt appointed Dr. Wiley to carry it out, and in the next six years the crusader established a firm basis of Federal control. That was when the courts began to get cases with such descriptive titles as *U.S. v. 935 Cases of Tomato Puree, U.S. v. Two Barrels of Desiccated Eggs,* and *U.S. v. 62 Packages of Marmola Tablets*—and rather uniformly found "for the people." Lethal foods and the worst excesses of the patent-medicine quacks disappeared. The 1906 act was amended and expanded—we now live under the Food, Drug and Cosmetic Act of 1967. Legal disputes in this field changed from defense of the right to sell poison to the proper limits of Federal regulation for ensuring informative labeling and safe products.

These regulations now permit the outright prohibition of foods containing additives that are strongly suspected of being dangerous. The danger may be slow in appearing too. The artificial chemical sweeteners known as cyclamates were greeted with joy by millions of weight-conscious Americans and others for whom sugar was a health hazard. Cyclamates haven't a calorie in a carload, and beginning in the 1950's, they were put into all sorts of diet foods and drinks. The sales were gratifyingly profitable even after the FDA issued a warning early in 1969 that the chemicals might have a laxative effect on steady consumers. But in the fall of that year, the results of laboratory studies of rats fed on food sweetened with cyclamates revealed a large incidence of cancer of the bladder. The announcement, coupled with the news that the rate of this disease among American men had doubled during the 1960's, led the FDA to order first a gradual withdrawal from the market of anything containing cyclamates, and then in 1970 a total ban on the chemical. The canning industry estimated that $30,000,000 worth of fruit had to be destroyed.

Whether or not the order could have been contested successfully on strictly legal grounds, no food processor was about to try. Victory, with the implication that the company demanded the right to sell a cancer-inducing product, could have been more disastrous than defeat. Yet the agency acted without waiting for definite proof that human beings had developed cancer after eating cyclamates or how much of the chemical constituted a dangerous dose. Law had reached the point where the serious chance of such a fearsome menace was enough to warrant imposing a severe loss upon a major segment of the economy.

Inspection is the key to enforcement of rules governing the quality of processed foods. Just how far the government may go in prying into private premises in search of health and sanitary violations is less clear now than it seemed in 1959 when Justice Felix Frankfurter wrote for himself and four of his colleagues an opinion in *Frank v. Maryland* from which Chief Justice Warren and three others dissented strongly. As so often is the case when large constitutional issues are resolved, the crime and the penalty were trivial. A Baltimore court found Frank guilty of a misdemeanor for refusing to let a city health inspector enter his house. The fine was $20. Frank contended he was within his rights; if the inspector wanted to get in, he should have a search warrant based on the Fourth Amendment's requirement of "probable cause, supported by oath or affirmation."

At the trial, the inspector testified that he surely had all the "probable cause" anyone could ask to suspect that the house was rat infested. In the backyard he saw a pile of about half a ton of trash mixed with rodent feces. He explained that he did not go downtown for a warrant because he had to release two students at 3 P.M., and be in his office by 3:30 to write his reports.

Justice Frankfurter, upholding the conviction, delved far back into English history to dredge up backing for his theory that the bar to illegal searches is designed as protection against self-incrimination. He then returned to Maryland to point out that the state's health inspection laws dated from 1801 when the fine for refusal to admit an inspector was the same as 150 years later—$20. In that span of time, he pointed out, new scientific knowledge confirmed the rationale for these inspections, and modern urban conditions heightened their importance. Since the search was "reasonable"—the Amendment forbids only "unreasonable" searches—Frank had not been deprived of due process of law. Justice Frankfurter added:

"Time and experience have forcefully taught that the power to inspect dwelling places, either as a matter of systematic area-by-area search or, as here, to treat a specific problem, is of indispensable importance to the maintenance of community health; a power that would be greatly hobbled by the blanket requirement of the safeguards necessary for a search of evidence of criminal acts. The need for preventive action is great, and city after city has seen this need and granted the power of inspection to its health officials; and these inspections are welcomed by all but an insignificant few."

Justice Douglas, writing for the four dissenters, went over the same ground in English history as Frankfurter but came up with the conclusion that the Fourth Amendment is not so much a protection against self-incrimination as it is "the common law right of a man to privacy in his home." He thought the inspector's reason for not taking time to get a warrant "flimsy ground" for denying this homeowner the constitutional protection of a search warrant. He pointed out that Baltimore carried out 28,000 to 36,000 inspections a year, but only once in twelve months, on the average, was anyone prosecuted for refusal to admit the inspector. "One rebel a year is not too great a price to pay for maintaining our guarantee of civil rights in full vigor," this dissent concluded.

Since inspectors have at least as great power to search without warrants in a food store or processing plant as in a home, *Frank* could have wide repercussions. In 1965, Congress strengthened the inspectors' power by authorizing seizure of suspected food or drugs without waiting for a court order. Inspections and seizures both multiplied. But the Supreme Court is quite capable of changing its mind. This time it waited only eight years to do so in a six-to-three decision:

"Having concluded that *Frank v. Maryland,* to the extent that it sanctions such warrantless inspections, must be overruled, we reverse."

The somersault was performed on June 5, 1967, in two cases from the Pacific Coast, *Camara v. Municipal Court of San Francisco* and *See v. City of Seattle.* In the first, an apartment house resident was arrested for refusing three times to let an inspector in without a warrant for a routine annual checkup. In the U. S. District Court, where he took his case after a municipal court convicted him, Camara argued that no "probable cause" existed as it had in *Frank.* The judge denied his plea on the ground that routine inspection was "part of a regulatory scheme which is essentially civil rather than criminal in nature," so Camara was not incriminating himself if he admitted the inspector. See had been fined $100 for blocking a routine fire department inspection of his locked warehouse, and the question here was whether commercial premises are any more or less sacred than a home.

Justice White handed down the reversal of the *Frank* decision, saying that while the searches were reasonable, the government must still have a warrant if a citizen objects. He pointed out in ruling against Camara that this should be easy to obtain because refusal to admit an inspector was "probable cause" for issuing a warrant. In the *See* opinion, he added that businessmen have the same rights as occupants of houses. The three dissenters thought the Court had been correct in 1959 (they had been part of that majority) and, of course, it could very well return to its former position.

Unless that happens, it appears inspectors for the Food and Drug Administration will have to get warrants if processors or store owners insist. So far as can be determined, the requirement has not discommoded officials in their work of seizing doubtful products. The safeguard for businessmen, furthermore, was strengthened when the New York State Liquor Authority tried to take away the license of Finn's Liquor Shop because the proprietor refused to admit an inspector. The Authority held that in accepting a government license to do business, a man tacitly consents to inspection. The state court disagreed: "No state may require as a condition of doing business, blanket submission to warrantless searches at any time and for any purpose." The Supreme Court, in refusing to review this case, indicated its approval of the principle.

A more difficult problem for Law, and for Science, too, is the amount of risk medicine and industry are justified in asking the public to run in order to get the benefits of new drugs. A powerful agent against some killing or crippling disease is discovered, and Law must say how long we wait to determine the side effects before letting doctors prescribe it for their patients. Law must also rule on the amount of testing to be done to be sure a drug does what the maker claims. Thanks to the enormous pharmaceutical advances of the last forty years, fewer than one in a dozen prescriptions today are for preparations known in the 1930's. This flood of new products has forced Law to take a new look at the Pure Food and Drug Act.

The chief prod to the reconsideration was sulfanilamide, one of the earliest "wonder drugs." In 1937, sulfanilamide dispensed by one manufacturer killed one hundred people. It turned out that he used as a solvent an antifreeze for automobile radiators. Congress amended the Act in 1938 to require submission of all new drugs to the Food and Drug Administration for approval before they could go on the market. Under this Act, manufacturers had to furnish details of what the new product contained and the results of any tests carried out in the laboratory or on animals or on people. The FDA was ordered to make its decision entirely on the basis of the information supplied by the manufacturer and not try to go beyond it or check it.

Thousands of applications and dozens of valuable new drugs later, some flaws in this procedure became apparent. Side effects were not researched adequately in the rush to get a useful remedy to the sick. Sometimes these effects were ignored when they became known. Law was slow to move in on these admittedly rare but sometimes deadly instances. A drug widely advertised to physicians as a specific for lowering the cholesterol level of their patients' blood turned out to cause falling hair and cataracts in some and a different but harmful fat in others. Yet it took two years to get the stuff withdrawn and then only after the FDA discovered that data on the manufacturer's original application had been falsified. Several hundred thousand patients had taken the medicine.

Another drug prescribed in more than 300,000 cases of

tuberculosis with no harmful side effects was discovered to be a useful "psychic energizer" to combat depression in mental patients. Many of the thousands for whom it was prescribed in the next two years contracted jaundice and at least fifteen of them died. Yet again it took nearly two more years to stop the use of the drug.

The clincher in this fight to reform the system of approving new drugs was a wave of horror caused in 1962 by a sedative, thalidomide, which, fortunately for Americans, was first marketed in Europe. There it proved disastrous for thousands of pregnant women, causing their babies to be born without arms or legs, or with other monstrous defects. Dr. Frances Kelsey of the FDA's medical staff won this country's highest civilian medal for blocking approval of the drug here. But meantime, 1,200 doctors had received a couple of million tablets to try on their patients without being told of the drug's dangers. The company instructed its salesmen to explain to physicians that they did not need to report the results because the basic research on the drug had been done, an implication that it had been proved safe.

The plight of women who took it but could not be legally aborted despite the known danger that they would bear armless, legless babies—in at least nine instances it happened—led to enormous public sympathy. One result was increased support for abortion reform. More immediately, Congress passed a new drug act that permitted the FDA to order a product withdrawn if it learned of dangers to public health and not wait for the damage to be done. Manufacturers were required to submit evidence by qualified investigators that a new product is safe and must include in all advertising a clear statement of known side effects. In 1967, Congress added that evidence of effectiveness in treating the condition for which a drug is to be used must also be provided.

In spite of all these safeguards, some risk remains. Not even the most searching investigation can be infallible, and someone will be damaged in spite of every known precaution. Law generally but not always holds the manufacturer or dispenser accountable even when no fault is imputed to him. The most notable exception has arisen in what are sometimes called "bad-blood cases."

One of these, cited all across the country, was a 1954 ruling by New York State's highest court. It held that Gussie Perlmutter could not collect from Beth David Hospital because a blood transfusion she received there carried an undetectable amount of infectious hepatitis, enough to give her the disease. A jury had awarded her $50,000 when her lawyers argued that in selling her the blood, the hospital implied that it was safe to use. Under the rule that a seller is responsible for his wares even when it is impossible for him to know they were defective, this was sound. But the seven judges who in New York have the last word ruled that transfusions are a service not a sale.

"The art of healing frequently calls for a balancing of risks and dangers to a patient," they added. "If injury results from the course adopted where no negligence or fault is present, liability should not be imposed upon the institution or agency actually seeking to save or otherwise assist the patient."

Thus, although a good many cases of hepatitis contracted during blood transfusions have been reported, the victims can collect only if they prove negligence. Many states adopted laws stating that the entire blood transaction is a service and never a sale, although money may pass. All the other states have judicial rulings similar to that in New York.

Most attempts to apply the same doctrine to drugs have failed. One of the first to plead the Perlmutter precedent was a leading pharmaceutical house that became a major producer of polio vaccine right after Dr. Jonas Salk's great discovery was pronounced both safe and effective on April 12, 1955. Within fifteen days, this one firm's vaccine was used for 400,000 safe injections. But a few doses contained live polio virus, although all were made in accordance with United States Public Health

Service specifications. As a result, 59 children contracted polio, and by 1956, forty suits for damages were brought on their behalf. The first two of these were tried in California. The facts were not disputed. The defendant cited *Perlmutter v. Beth David Hospital* as a reason why a blameless manufacturer should not be held liable. The trial judge, however, charged the jury that if they found the children were infected by the vaccine, the doctrine of implied warranty applied. This was in line with Cardozo's revolutionary principle, described in Chapter 1, that a customer is entitled to rely upon a manufacturer to make a safe product. The jurors, although they said later they thought this was unfair, awarded $125,000 to one child and $14,000 to another less seriously afflicted. One of the twelve refused to go along with the verdict in spite of the judge's charge, but California does not require unanimity in juries trying civil suits. In 1960, the state Supreme Court upheld the awards. The opinion specifically rejected the New York precedent, pointing out that the California legislature had relieved blood of any implied warranty. If the lawmakers meant to do the same for drugs, they would have to say so. The Court also managed to distinguish the two cases, saying vaccine was more like food, since it was meant to be "introduced into the human body." But, of course, blood is also so introduced in a transfusion. Although no judge said so, the interpretation often placed on these decisions is that a company is better able to bear the money costs of a tragedy than individuals. The Salk vaccine maker finally settled the claims for a total of about $4,000,000.

The courts seem slightly more anxious to protect the public's health than its pocketbook. In 1966, two suits against government regulation were taken up in the same term of the Supreme Court—*Abbott Laboratories et al v. Gardner et al* and *Toilet Goods Association et al v. Gardner et al*. In the first case, the plaintiffs were 37 manufacturers, who made 90 percent of all prescription drugs sold in this country, and their trade association. They wanted the court to set aside an FDA regulation requiring every mention of a drug's proprietary or brand name to be accompanied, in type at least half as large, by the generic name, which is always much cheaper. Thus, pills marketed as Miltown or Equanil would have to be labeled also as meprobamate. The Toilet Goods Association and its members asked annulment of another regulation. This one stated that if FDA employes were denied access to any process in the preparation of color additives, the FDA would not certify the product as safe. This meant it could not be marketed. The Gardner named was Secretary of Health, Education and Welfare John W. Gardner and the "et al" were the responsible officials under him.

The government did not want to argue the merits of the cases at all. It held that the plaintiffs should be thrown out of court until they could show some evidence that they had been damaged. This is the old argument of "standing," and the issue here was when does a government agency's ruling become ripe for judicial review. In the pharmaceutical case, the court decided that it was ripe now because if the manufacturers had to print all those generic names in big type, they would go to considerable expense before they learned whether the agency order was justified. So the issue should go back to the lower courts for a determination of the order's validity.

Justice Abe Fortas dissented on the ground that this was what he called a "shotgun" attempt to block agency action and should not be condoned. Justice Tom C. Clark also dissented, but apparently because he thought the FDA order should be declared valid then and there. Some personal feeling crept into his opinion as he described a recent experience in paying ten times as much for trade-name eyedrops and twelve times as much for a drug as he should have for the unbranded article. He accused his brethren of "sabotaging the public interest" and concluded:

"Rather than crying over the plight that the laboratories

have brought upon themselves, the Court should think more of the poor folks who suffer under this practice."

The same day, the Court acceded to the government's request and threw out the Toilet Goods case. In this instance, they said, the plaintiffs would not be hurt if they had to wait until one of them actually was denied a certification before they were heard. Furthermore, this concerned nothing that anyone was going to swallow or have injected, and Law usually is a little less rigid in handling substances that go on rather than into the body.

The net result of all this legislation and litigation is that Law has made considerable strides toward achieving a balance between risks and benefits acceptable to the public. Pharmaceutical spokesmen are often heard to deplore the stricter regulations as diminishing their laboratories' incentive to experiment. They profess to fear so heavy a burden will stop their looking for better medicines. Yet when they check out their own risks versus benefits, they find that the pot of gold at the end of the rainbow of a new healing drug is too alluring to forgo. It is a fairly safe prediction that Law will hold them to greater rather than less accountability despite their protests.

16 | Science,
Law and Crime

Science has forged powerful weapons against crime, and criminals turn some of them successfully against society. But scientific detection of offenders is not especially modern; it has been going on almost as long as history. A famous scientific discovery of antiquity, the one that had Archimedes leaping from his bath to run down the street shouting "Eureka!" was made while he was trying to solve a crime around 215 B.C. His patron and kinsman, Hiero, the Tyrant of Syracuse, suspected that his new, supposedly solid-gold crown was part silver. He ordered Archimedes to learn the truth without scratching the surface or chipping off a piece.

The problem seemed insoluble until it occurred to the great mathematician while in his tub that he could tell because the density, or specific gravity, of gold is different from that of silver, and a mixture of the two different from either. This could be determined without marring the crown. Archimedes proceeded to work out the principle for this test. Since all solid objects weigh less under water than in air, their density can be calculated by dividing the weight in air by the weight of the water it displaces. The figure for gold is 19.3 grams per milliliter, for silver 10.5. Archimedes was able to ascertain not only that the crown contained silver but the exact proportion. One legend has it that Hiero executed the goldsmith who made the crown.

More recently, Science has provided the crime laboratory with increasingly sophisticated apparatus—the electron microscope, spectograph, X-ray equipment, infrared and ultraviolet light, voice prints, and many assorted marvels of physics and chemistry. Nearly all are admittedly proper tools of the crime detection trade and are employed without argument at the discretion of the police.

Law's unquestioning acceptance of most of them has been a by-product of the public's general reverence for technology. But it was not always so. Defense lawyers used to argue heatedly to exclude evidence obtained by means of newfangled tricks. Fingerprints were not firmly established as proof of identity in criminal trials in this country, until 1911, although the technique was nearly 2,500 years old, having been used in China instead of seals on documents. As is often the case, the first American use of technology to solve a crime was fictional, with Mark Twain's Pudd'nhead Wilson solving a murder in 1893. Law was called upon in real life when Thomas Jennings was being tried for killing a Chicago householder during a burglary in 1911. Fingerprints were found in some paint spread in the house only that day. Jennings' lawyer tried to prevent experts from testifying that the prints in the paint exactly matched those of the defendant. The trial judge admitted the evidence; Jennings appealed, and the Illinois Supreme Court affirmed his conviction, saying:

"From the evidence in the record, we are disposed to hold that the classification of fingerprint impressions is a science."

In the generally accredited armory of weapons that technology offers in the war on crime, two sets of tools still call for special legislation and have inspired innumerable court contests. The legality of using either is still debated warmly. Neither legislators nor judges are unanimous in appraising the merits of the argument. One horn of this legal dilemma is formed by the increasingly delicate and perceptive methods for listening to a suspect and even watching him anywhere he may be. The other is made up of a variety of drugs or techniques to induce truthful talk, expose a lie, or reveal such intimate facts as how much alcohol an automobile driver has in his blood.

Our society has always regarded eavesdropping as a dirty business, even when it is legitimate. In this country, wiretapping and "bugging" a man's home or office to overhear or record his conversations have been repeatedly outlawed by statute and condemned by the courts. Law enforcement officers must get a court order, the equivalent of a search warrant, before they can legally engage in the practice. They do a great deal of it without getting permission, and it gives them opportunities for both arrests and shakedowns.

Law's only serious attempt to discourage unauthorized electronic snooping by policemen is to forbid them to use the evidence in a trial. The rules established for the Federal judiciary have long excluded the fruits of any illegal investigations. But many states allowed the testimony. The different circumstances under which this was permitted, approved in one state and rejected in another, may seem frustrating to those who like universal rules. But Law is not always bound by the virtue of small minds' consistency. Variety on introducing "tainted" evidence in court has given us a chance to try out several different theories of Law in this field and adapt to the particular judgments and prejudices prevailing in various states. Until 1961, the states were free to follow their own rules. Today that is no longer true in certain kinds of crime—just what kind seems to depend upon the Supreme Court's degree of outrage at the time it is reviewed.

Three Cleveland policemen launched Law's search for clarification on May 23, 1957, when they went to the home of Miss Dollree Mapp on the second floor of a two-family house. They had a tip that they would find gambling paraphernalia and a person wanted for questioning in connection with a bombing. Miss Mapp, who was involved in civil litigation at the time, told them to wait while she called her lawyer. He advised her to admit the men only if they had a search warrant. The three called police headquarters and settled down to watch. Three hours later, four more policemen arrived, but Miss Mapp still refused to open the door, and they broke in, finding her standing on the stairs. When she demanded to see their warrant, one of them held up a piece of paper. She seized it and thrust it into her bosom. In the struggle to get it back, the policemen handcuffed her, took back the paper and forced her into her apartment. Meantime her lawyer had arrived, but they would not let him in. They searched the whole apartment, finding neither the person they wanted to question nor any gambling evidence. However, in the basement they came across what was later described as "four little pamphlets, a couple of photographs, and a little pencil doodle" that they judged to be obscene. In due course, Miss Mapp was convicted of possessing this pornography, although she and a friend both testified that the things had been left by a former boarder who had moved to New York. The prosecution did not pretend the piece of paper the policemen showed was a warrant and indeed made no mention of it.

The Ohio Supreme Court, to which Miss Mapp appealed, doubted that any warrant ever was issued and called the police methods repugnant to a sense of justice. But the judges did not think the actual "obscene" evidence on which she was convicted was seized from Miss Mapp's person "by the use of brutal or offensive physical force." They also cited a United States Supreme Court ruling of 1949, *Wolf v. Colorado*, which held that the Fourteenth Amendment did not bar states from using illegally acquired evidence. Miss Mapp's counsel asked the Supreme Court to reconsider their recognition of variety's value in the rules of evidence. Counsel also wanted the Ohio law that you can be jailed for keeping a dirty book in your own home for your own pleasure declared unconstitutional. The nine judges in Washington, who heard arguments in 1961, did not offer an opinion on this last point because they could dispose of the case without getting into a hassle over pornography. Six of them concluded:

"We hold that all evidence obtained by searches and seizures in violation of the Constitution is, by that same authority, inadmissible in a state court."

As to the 1949 decision that the Ohio court relied upon, it had been handed down when at least two-thirds of the states allowed testimony of this kind. Since then, the Federal rule had been adopted more or less in most states (not Ohio) because, as California's highest tribunal had said, "other remedies have completely failed to secure compliance with the constitutional provisions." The states had had plenty of time to mend their rules. Justice Hugo L. Black, who had been in the 1949 majority, wrote a concurring opinion to explain why he had changed his mind. He now thought that the Fifth Amendment safeguard against self-incrimination applied since the illegally seized evidence was the defendant's own papers. The three dissenters held that the 1949 decision was correct, that the Supreme Court supervised Federal tribunals and police procedures but not those of the states.

Two years later, in 1963, the same judge who wrote the Mapp opinion, Justice Clark, spoke for the court to pronounce a California search of George and Diane Ker's apartment reasonable and lawful, although the police had no warrant. The raiders found marijuana, and the Kers were convicted of possessing it. They asked the Supreme Court to rule that the conviction had to be set aside because no one had a right to conduct a warrantless search on mere suspicion. Justice Clark noted that detectives had seen Ker with a recently released dealer from whom, according to an informant, Ker had purchased marijuana. Without bothering to get a warrant, the detectives borrowed a key from the building superintendent and quietly let themselves in so that, they explained, the Kers would not have time to destroy the evidence. Under California law, they were allowed to break in after they said who they were and what they wanted. Justice Clark and four others on the high bench thought state law should govern these cases unless the Federal Constitution is offended.

"We find no such offensiveness in the facts here," he concluded.

Four justices preferred to apply *Mapp*. A constitutional principle was at stake, they pointed out, not a question of police courtesy.

These two cases suggest that in dealing with eavesdropping in all its myriad forms, the Supreme Court's reaction to state use of the fruits may depend more upon the manner than the matter of the surveillance. Federal authorities, except in investigations involving foreign espionage and kidnapping, have been held to a stricter rule. But the Omnibus Crime Control and Safe Streets Act of 1968 applies to all, Federal or local. This imposes a $10,000 fine or five years imprisonment on anyone who intercepts, discloses or uses in any way the wire or oral communications of another. Any person aggrieved by a violation is also entitled to damages, recoverable in a civil suit. The Supreme Court has held that this means only the person whose communication was actually overheard, not a third party who may have been "aggrieved" by what someone else said during the intercepted conversation. Policemen have tapped thousands of telephones and "bugged" thousands of rooms since then, but the record does not disclose a conviction, although Justice Byron R. White commented shortly after the act was passed:

"Without experience showing the contrary, we should not assume that the new statute will be cavalierly disregarded or will not be enforced against transgressors."

Under the Omnibus Crime Act and its predecessor, private citizens have gone to jail or been fined for wiretapping and bugging. Policemen and prosecutors have not. The deterrent to their unauthorized eavesdropping—decreasingly effective—has been to bar from any trial other evidence found as a result of the wiretap. But before this can be done, someone has to know that official wrongdoing turned up the evidence. As technology develops ever more sensitive devices, it becomes possible for an electronically equipped eavesdropper to record the conversation of two men whispering to each other in the middle of a field out of sight. The notion, widely held among prosecutors and others, that the government is privileged to play the record in a courtroom still offends most members of the Supreme Court. Of course, the police use information so obtained to find other admissible evidence, and then we never hear of the eavesdropping.

The Supreme Court's 1967 pronouncement on the subject is often cited to support arguments that law enforcement agencies should get out of the dirty business. The FBI, busily trying to suppress a Federal crime—transmitting wagering information by telephone across state lines—attached one of the new, sensitive bugs on top of a telephone booth in Los Angeles used by Charles Katz, whom they suspected of communicating for betting purposes with Boston and Miami. They neither tapped the lines nor physically invaded Katz's privacy inside the booth but simply listened comfortably at a distance. Their defense was that they had good reason to believe they would overhear gambling transactions, and their bug was in a public place outside anyone's constitutionally protected premises.

The District Court and the Court of Appeals agreed with the agents, but the Supreme Court, with Justice Black dissenting, said all were wrong. The mere fact that the agents had reason to suspect a crime did not make their action "reasonable" within the meaning of the Fourth Amendment, the justices pointed out. Warrants should have been obtained. As to the argument that the agents did not enter any area occupied by Katz but kept to public domain, the opinion countered that this was irrelevant. Relying on previous decisions, courts had been ruling that a "spike mike" driven into an outside wall an eighth of an inch was an illegal "penetration" of private premises, but a "stethoscope mike," merely pressed against the wall, was permissible. Science's advance in electronic gadgetry now drove Law to take account of reality, and the Katz decision abolished the distinction. It said:

"For the Fourth Amendment protects people, not places. . . . One who occupied it [the booth], shuts the door behind him, and pays the toll that permits him to place a call is surely entitled to assume that the words he utters into the mouthpiece will not be broadcast to the world. . . . The Government's activities . . . violated the privacy upon which he justifiably relied . . . and thus constituted a 'search and seizure' within the meaning of the Fourth Amendment."

Need the FBI be so circumspect when it investigates a more serious crime? Kidnapping and foreign espionage are exempted from restrictions, but the Federal judiciary has not been willing to relax the rule for anything else, even when the Attorney General of the United States certifies a need for surveillance. Amid the domestic turmoil of the last few years, with assorted radicals of all shades of political opinion indulging in reckless violence, the Executive Branch of the government became sufficiently alarmed to dispense with court orders. It advanced and operated on the theory that this was justified "to protect the nation from attempts of domestic organizations to attack and subvert the existing structure of government."

The quoted words are from a 1970 affidavit by Attorney General John N. Mitchell explaining an unauthorized wiretap. It was installed to expose what he said was a conspiracy to blow up an office of the Central Intelligence Agency in Ann Arbor, Michigan. It was the first time the government's top lawman had ever intervened openly in a surveillance case involving purely domestic "violent disorders." The man whose conversations were recorded was Lawrence R. Plamondon, a so-called White Panther, one of three accused of the plot. Mitchell had condoned the tap without bothering a judge. He insisted that this was an "inherent power" of the government. While Mitchell did not plead the precedent, Robert Kennedy as Attorney General had given the FBI a green light on wiretaps without court orders. But Kennedy was careful not to publicize the fact. In January 1971, the District Court in Detroit ruled that Mitchell's "inherent power" did not exist; the Attorney General and the FBI have no more right to break the law than anyone else.

The government appealed, and on April 8 the Court of Appeals in Cincinnati upheld the ruling. By two to one, it reported that it was unable to find any wording in the Constitution that supported Mitchell's view of his power. It noted that President Truman had pleaded the same "inherent power" during the Korean War when he ordered the country's steel mills seized, an action the Supreme Court found illegal.

The decision, of course, does not forbid FBI wiretapping any more than earlier decisions forbid searches of suspects' homes. It merely said that the Constitution establishes the courts, not the Attorney General, as the agency for authorizing taps. The distinction is by no means a quibble. It is part of the system that keeps prosecutors and policemen from becoming the judges of the offenders against whom they have a case. On the other hand, the rules of procedure for the Federal courts do not specifically empower the judges to issue warrants to tap telephones.

Wiretapping is only one part of electronic surveillance, and according to some experienced law enforcement officers, it's an inefficient one because it wastes a lot of time and seldom turns up genuinely useful information against criminals that could not be found much more easily by older police methods. It does reveal information that can serve a blackmailer or an industrial spy or just prove plain embarrassing. More likely to get results is an electronic device attached to an informer who leads a suspect into incautious talk recorded at a distance by the informer's confederate. Since one party to the conversation agrees to this, it is legal, although not very nice.

To many people, objections to wiretapping and bugging are part of the modern coddling of criminals. Would an honest man have anything to hide? they ask. The answer is that most honest men do, and few would talk freely to anyone if they knew a policeman was taking down every word. More objectionable, electronic eavesdropping gives the listener all sorts of leads that have nothing to do with crime—business secrets, confidential information on the market or sports events, indiscretions of people who may or may not be involved in the suspected crime. J. Edgar Hoover once said he would not want the FBI to have authority to install its taps. He explained that he would be afraid of becoming the director of a gang of blackmailers. The danger is not so much that the tapper would sell out to the suspect but that he would hear the secrets of third parties that had nothing to do with the official investigation.

As eavesdropping techniques become ever more refined and pervasive, Law may consider enforcing the penal clauses of the statutes instead of merely barring the evidence from trials. She may also develop acceptable authorizations other than a court order. A proctor appointed by the Supreme Court to oversee wiretap activities of Federal agencies would be one such device.

Incidentally, Law's supposed coddling of criminals by protecting their constititutional rights is a mirage. Those freed by "legal technicalities" are a small fraction of the total number of persons arrested who never come to trial. A survey in the District of Columbia revealed that for every suspect who was released because he had been tapped or was not warned of his rights or was refused a lawyer or signed a forced confession, seven were dismissed because the time between arrest and trial was so long that witnesses disappeared or forgot, material evidence was lost, or complainants grew weary. "Delay is the best witness for the defense" is an old lawyers' maxim, so it is not surprising that most delays are sought by the accused and his counsel.

On the other hand, the Department of Justice has reported that in the first two years of Mitchell's term, 1969 and 1970, it had operated 253 electronic surveillances with court approval. These led to 800 arrests involving organized crime and 72 convictions. This is a ratio of 9 convictions per 100 arrests as compared to 70 out of 100 for all adults charged with the serious crimes the FBI uses to compile its index telling us whether crime is increasing or decreasing. Although this is hardly a good testimonial for wiretapping as a police tool, twelve states authorize it under court order and more are expected to do so.

Science's other controversial contribution to crime detection is in the search for truth. Drugs that induce uninhibited revelations, chemical analysis that reveals the proportion of alcohol in blood, and the lie detector have obvious value in exposing the guilty and equally obvious danger in trapping the innocent. Law has been extremely cautious in permitting juries to hear information obtained as a result of the polygraph or "truth serum," but is more receptive to the blood test.

The uses and abuses of drugs that short-circuit human inhibitions are well-illustrated in three quite different cases that puzzled the courts one way or another. Perhaps the conclusion to be drawn from them is that Science must become more exact in this field before Law can define her rules precisely.

The simplest of the three cases was tried in Washington, D. C. in 1954. A young woman accused a soldier of breaking into her home and raping her, a charge he denied. They were the only two witnesses and agreed on only one point—they were strangers to each other. Both seemed honest and made a good impression. The judge suggested they allow themselves to be injected with "truth serum." Under its influence, the soldier repeated his original story. The girl told of being so bitter against men that she picked the soldier at random and invented the rape story to get revenge on the sex.

In Chicago during 1945 and 1946, William Heirens, a 17-year-old university student, killed at least two women and a little girl, attacked several others, and committed about three hundred burglaries in a one-man crime wave that for a time thoroughly terrorized the South Side. When he was finally caught escaping from an apartment, he was knocked unconscious. The police took his fingerprints while he was still insensible and learned that they matched impressions found on the doorjamb of the little girl's room. He still had not opened his eyes, but the doctors thought he was faking and gave him a dose of one of the truth drugs to bring him out of his coma. He promptly confessed to the murders and the long list of burglaries, gave details no innocent man could have learned, and told where much of the loot was stored.

At his trial, his lawyers tried to exclude the evidence resulting from this confession on the ground that his constitutional rights had been violated. The prosecutor did not defend the practice of getting truth by means of drugs. He argued that the doctors were not trying to make Heirens incriminate himself but to restore him to consciousness. The court accepted this, and Heirens' appeal failed.

Later the Supreme Court ruled out just such testimony even when the drug was purportedly administered for another reason than to get a confession. This was in a murder trial, too, but the final verdict came only after the high bench had considered the case on five separate occasions and heard it fully argued twice in the nine years that elapsed between arrest and decision. This appeal, too, came up from Chicago where the marathon began on New Year's Eve, 1953.

A probationer picked up that night as a robbery suspect told the police he had seen a 19-year-old heroin addict named

Charles Townsend carrying a brick not far from where Jack Boone, a steelworker, had been robbed and killed by a heavy blow two weeks earlier. A few hours later, the police found Townsend, obviously drugged, and locked him in a cell all through the day and far into the next night. At times, they questioned him, and he denied having anything to do with Boone. He was taken out briefly to a lineup to see if another robbery victim could identify him, but the victim picked someone else. Back in his cell, Townsend began suffering the usual agonizing withdrawal symptoms, and a police doctor gave him an injection of phenobarbital and scopolamine, the latter a common truth drug. The dose not only relieved the addict's anguish but set him talking so fast that in nine minutes he dictated a confession to the Boone killing, three other murders, and two robberies, including the one whose victim had not recognized him. At his trial, the confession was all the evidence the state had. Townsend testified not only that it was false but that he could not remember making it. The informer's story was hardly relevant since he was unable to say what day of the week he had seen Townsend with the brick.

During six years of appeals through the state and Federal courts, the nine men in Washington twice refused to listen. On a third appeal, they ordered a district judge to determine if a Federal case existed. Finally, in 1961, they agreed to review this judge's ruling to let the Illinois verdict stand because it followed state procedures. Only seven justices were present and could not muster five votes for a decision. They set reargument for 1962, and on March 18, 1963, Chief Justice Earl Warren delivered an opinion that quashed the conviction for good.

By this time, Townsend had been tried and acquitted of one other murder to which he had admitted during his "confession." The prosecutor had never bothered to transcribe the account of a third killing because it was too vague to make much sense. All charges in the fourth had been dropped when witnesses turned up to say the dead man had attributed his fatal injuries to an accident. Both robbery counts were also dismissed since the victims had identified others as the culprits.

This record seemed to the Supreme Court to throw a good deal of doubt on Townsend's confession to killing Boone. But the Chief Justice's main point was that drug-induced admissions to crime are worthless because in our system of justice any valid confession must be "the product of a rational intellect and a free will." He concluded:

"It is difficult to imagine a situation in which a confession would be less the product of a free intellect, less voluntary, than when brought about by a drug having the effect of a 'truth serum.' "

This was a five-to-four decision. The minority did not defend the use of drugs, but would not interfere with an Illinois rule that makes a trial judge the final authority on admissibility of confessions. This dissent held that the Federal system gives states a right to make their own rules so long as these do not violate specific mandates of the United States Constitution. The closeness of the decision and the continuing search for scientific means to combat crime suggest that another nine justices, confronted with a similar case, would reverse the Townsend decision.

In view of the large number of automobile accidents involving drivers who have imbibed alcohol, the determination of just how much a particular suspect's faculties were impaired by drink is a key issue in innumerable instances. At various times, police have watched him try to walk a straight line, listened to him repeat a tricky sentence, smelled his breath, and measured the alcoholic content of his breath as exhaled into a bag. Eventually, Science convinced Law that a blood test is more accurate than other methods, and that at 0.15 milliliters of alcohol to 100 milliliters of blood, no one has complete control of his car. A policeman's right to demand and to take a blood sample has been contested bitterly; the contests get into court only when the driver fails to pass the test. The question is whether the statutes designed to punish drunken drivers can be constitutionally enforced by drawing off blood against a man's will. The Supreme Court has answered it several times.

Before any blood cases reached this high level, lower court judges ruled that the police could not do it, although the state was privileged to forfeit a driver's license if he failed to give the sample "voluntarily." Judges usually cited as their authority a Supreme Court decision, *Rochin v. California* (1952), which upset a narcotics conviction. State police broke into Rochin's home, and when he popped something into his mouth, rushed him to a hospital and had his stomach pumped. Morphine tablets thus recovered were the basis of his conviction. The court said this method of obtaining evidence of a crime "shocked the conscience," "is bound to offend even hardened sensibilities," and is also unconstitutional for this reason:

"It would be a stultification of the responsibility which the course of constitutional history has cast upon this Court to hold that in order to convict a man the police cannot extract by force what is in his mind but can extract what is in his stomach."

On the strength of this, Paul Breithaupt, serving a sentence for manslaughter in New Mexico, appealed to have his conviction reversed. He had been injured in a motor vehicle accident in which three other people were killed. A jury believed he had been drunk at the time because his blood had more than a 0.15 alcoholic content, according to a technician. Breithaupt had been unconscious in the hospital emergency room when a policeman asked an attending physician for a blood sample and got it. In 1957, six Supreme Court justices decided this was legal, drawing a distinction between pumping out a man's stomach while he consciously resists and taking a little blood while he is unaware of it. All the people's concern for safety on the roads justified the slight intrusion on his privacy. Three dissenters saw no difference that mattered in getting such evidence by stealth or by force.

By 1966, the whole Court had come around to the conclusion that no essential difference exists. But now five members justified force as well as stealth in getting blood. This new majority argued that the procedure did not really compel a driver to be a witness against himself, and as a "search" it was "reasonable." The three who had dissented in *Breithaupt* held to their former opinion and were joined by a new member of the Court.

All nine were considering the plight of Armando Schmerber, who also had been hurt in an automobile accident and whose blood was taken by a physician in the hospital at the request of a policeman. But Schmerber had been conscious and protested vigorously to no avail. The trial judge admitted the analysis of his blood, showing that he was drunk, and Schmerber appealed his conviction, which carried a jail sentence of thirty days and a $250 fine. The Supreme Court majority pointed out that although the Fifth Amendment protects the accused from being compelled to testify against himself or to provide incriminating evidence, taking a blood sample did not compel him to do or say anything. The analogy, as they saw it, is to taking his fingerprints or forcing him to put on a hat when he is being identified by witnesses who never saw him bareheaded.

No such opinions from this highest of judicial bodies have clarified Law's attitude toward the lie detector. Lower courts refuse to allow polygraph experts to testify unless both sides agree in advance. Some judges have refused to allow either side to change its mind; others have ruled that this is permissible at any time before the expert actually testifies.

Outside the courtroom, the lie detector has been used (and abused) to turn up evidence or force a confession that is admissible at a trial. An ironic example was related by Erle Stanley Gardner in *The Court of Last Resort*, which describes how he and a panel of specialists investigated instances of what they considered possible miscarriages of justice in real life. One was the conviction of a young Ohioan for murder. The victim had been killed with a revolver of the same caliber as a weapon the condemned man owned. A ballistics expert's testimony was so complex and confusing that the jury clearly thought he said the bullet could have come from the defendant's gun when he actually had determined that it could not. As part of Gardner's investigation, he had a polygraph expert give the prisoner a lie detector test. The writer expected this to confirm the plea of innocence. Instead, it revealed that the man was guilty. He deliberately shot his victim with another gun and then subtly led police to his own, knowing that a ballistics test would show it had not fired the fatal bullet.

Because polygraph evidence is admitted only by agreement, relatively few court decisions have been recorded concerning it, and most of these are from trial courts. One of the rare appeals opinions, still referred to as perhaps the most comprehensive judicial review of the subject, was handed down by the Arizona Supreme Court in *State v. Valdez* in 1962. The five judges took the case at the request of the trial court, which asked for another opinion because the problem was new in their state. Prosecution and defense had agreed to have a man accused of narcotics law violations take a lie detector test. The results reflected badly on him, and he wanted them kept from the jury, but they were admitted and he was found guilty.

The state Supreme Court went back to 1923, only two years after the first police use of a polygraph in Berkeley, California, to find the earliest court record. In *Frye v. U.S.*, a District of Columbia judge refused to admit lie detector evidence that a second degree murder defendant was telling the truth. (While he was serving a life sentence, the real murderer confessed.) In New York City in 1938, the trial judge admitted testimony by a polygraph expert on behalf of the defense in *People v. Kenny*, a murder trial, over the objection of the prosecution. But later that year, the New York Court of Appeals in

People v. Forte upheld exclusion of such testimony under similar circumstances.

The Arizona review cited three other appellate court rulings, all rejecting lie-detector results as evidence. The first came from Kansas in 1941, *State v. Lowry.* The trial judge had suggested that Lowry and the chief witness against him take lie detector tests. The result led to his conviction, which the appellate judges canceled, saying the evaluation of polygraph readings "seems quite too subtle a task to impose upon an untrained jury." The other two appellate opinions were delivered in 1950. The California Appeals Court held that the technique was not sufficiently scientific to be mentioned in a courtroom and reversed a murder conviction in *People v. Wochnick.* In North Dakota in *State v. Pusch,* the offer of lie detector testimony had been made by the defense and was disallowed.

The unanimity for rejecting lie detector evidence to which either side objects does not prevail when one party tries to have the result excluded after stipulating that it should be received. The first case of this kind, *LeFevre v. State,* came to the Wisconsin Supreme Court in 1943. The district attorney went back on his agreement after the test favored the defendant, and the trial judge upheld an objection to the evidence. The state Supreme Court said this was quite proper but upset the conviction on other grounds. In *People v. Houser,* a California sex crime trial of 1948, the defense sought the exclusion. After agreeing to let the results be told to the jury, Houser objected that the expert was not qualified. The appeals court said the evidence was admissible because both sides had consented; the defendant should have questioned the expert's qualifications before making the agreement. The Michigan Supreme Court in 1951 ruled out polygraph evidence whether by agreement or order of a judge. The case under review, *Stone v. Earp,* involved the ownership of a trailer truck. The trial judge ordered both claimants to take a lie detector test, and after hearing the expert, awarded the truck to Earp. The higher court said "such tests do not attain the status of competent evidence," and the judge should have found for Earp on the basis of the valid testimony he had heard. The Iowa Supreme Court ruled in 1960 that polygraph evidence was properly admitted in a murder trial, *State v. McNamara,* over defense objections because the defense had stipulated acceptance in advance. In 1961, the New Mexico Supreme Court held in reversing an incest conviction, *State v. Trimble,* that no agreement between defense and prosecution could validate this sort of evidence.

After this elaborate survey, the Arizona judges decided that the lie detector is reliable enough in the hands of a qualified expert to be used if both sides agree and the trial court believes the test was fairly conducted. They added that the expert should be available for cross examination, and the judge should charge the jury that the polygraph does not reveal guilt or innocence of this particular crime but only whether the subject told the truth when he took the test.

Although the public generally is impressed by lie detection, the question of how severely witnesses or defendants should be pressed to submit to it remains open. For about twenty years before 1959, some of Chicago's municipal judges virtually ordered the tests in both civil and criminal cases where a direct conflict between the word of two witnesses was a key point. Either side had the right to refuse, but most lawyers considered it risky to offend the judge by doing so even when they believed it would be unfair to their clients; the technique is not infallible even when used by highly trained examiners, and the vast majority are not. Few protests to the Chicago practice appeared in open court, but remonstrances reached the legislature, which, in 1959, adopted a statute barring judicial mention of the idea in any criminal case.

Of course, outside Law, the lie detector remains a powerful police weapon. It can be used to undermine a story told stubbornly (and sometimes truthfully) no matter what the machine records. Once in a while, such uses are exposed in court. *The Great Fall* by Mildred Savage, which won the Mystery Writers of America award for the best fact crime book of 1970, chronicled such an instance in Connecticut. Lie detectors applied by unscrupulous detectives induced a not very bright young man to confess to a murder he had not committed. He was convicted on the basis of the confession, but during a second trial, the lie detector transcript was played back for the defense. The confession was thrown out, and the whole prosecution case collapsed.

No doubt Law will receive other new scientific methods for learning the truth as gingerly as she does drugs and lie detectors. She may soon be confronted with the perfection of mental telepathy or hypnosis or the invention of an electronic device that transcribes a man's thoughts by eavesdropping on his brainwaves. Then every witness could be read like a book in court before he ever opens his mouth. As it is and has been in this country, Law would reject this certainty to retain the tradition that the state must bear the burden of proving guilt.

Much more dangerous is the force of public opinion, which holds a man guilty if he declines to subject himself to the test of hypnotism or electronics or whatever gadget may come along to expose his innermost secrets. It seems improbable that Law would reach this position unless the people, whose will she ultimately reflects, abandon any desire for privacy in thought or deed.

Law's confused gropings for sound rules on the scientific devices already discussed in this chapter foreshadow her difficulties in regulating the even more sophisticated technology of the future. She will need state-by-state fumbling for workable solutions to problems such as responsibility for posthypnotic crimes and who should be licensed to read people's minds. Until the various possibilities are tested in the crucible of Federalism's fifty laboratories, the true values and hazards will not be known.

17 | Law and the Computer

In not much more than twenty-five years, a machine that most of us never see has changed our lives and ways of doing things profoundly and so rapidly that the effects are only imperfectly known. The computer, first produced in 1946 and introduced to business in 1954, makes possible our present systems of credit, merchandising, manufacturing, transportation, research, education, dissemination of information, government, and politics. It has revolutionized all these by its ability to store virtually limitless amounts of data of all kinds in very little space and give any part of it back on demand in seconds.

It creates situations for Law that could never arise when facts and figures had to be kept on paper in files put together by human hands. This imposed strict limits on the volume of information any organization, even a government, could profitably collect. Dossiers on individuals and groups had to be relatively few, for only thousands could be handled by a staff that had to write and file every detail. The computer changed all that. It can digest as many details about as many subjects as its programmer orders. In the process, it has nudged George Orwell's fanciful prophecy, *1984,* toward reality.

Orwell imagined a society in which "Big Brother" knew everything about everybody. As the computer permits us to approach this level of omniscience, "Big Brother" may be the government. He may also be a credit company, an association of employers, a vigilante group, a band of patriots or scoundrels dedicated to preserving their own brand of politics, religion, or morals, or indeed anyone with a highly developed curiosity about his fellowman.

In this country, Law has two methods of handling litigation that hinges on the knowledge men have about each other. Small-town practice differs from that in big cities. Where everyone knows everyone else and may be related to most, no lawyer would seek a jury of strangers to try his client. The panel is expected to be familiar with all concerned in the case. This was the original intent of the jury system—men tried by other men who knew them, not by some agent of the sovereign who was a stranger. In a big city, the ideal juryman never heard of the case or anyone remotely connected with it. Both systems have their merits. In the small town, a man's information about his neighbors is firsthand. In the city, he learns about litigation and litigants from newspapers. When it comes to privacy, Law's small-town and big-city attitudes are equally divergent. What is an intolerable intrusion to a city dweller who is unacquainted with anyone living near him is mere neighborliness to the householder who is very well-acquainted with everyone he is likely to see on the street.

In both situations, at the very least, the computer forces Law to review its stand on the individual's right of privacy. Who is entitled to collect and store information about a citizen? Under what conditions? Does the citizen have a right to know what the computer has on him or about him? Should he be allowed to correct errors? Who is entitled to receive the information? To what uses may the receiver put it? Is the receiver or the computer's owner or the supplier of information responsible for damages to the citizen if the facts are wrong? If they are correct?

To these conundrums, Law gives only the vaguest answers, most of them derived from a simpler day's laws governing privacy, libel, slander, and disclosure. For instance, if you can prove that the computer lied about you and also that some human malice was behind the falsehood—the machine is incapable of malice—you have redress. You may win under other circumstances too. One businessman, bankrupted in 1962 by such erroneous information released by a credit-rating firm, won a damage suit in 1969 without proving malice. The award was $6,610,000, big even in the field of big business litigation, but appeals could whittle it down or cancel it.

Few cases, however, are so clearcut as this one. The analogy is often to the classic story used to puzzle law students. A man throws a lighted squib out of a window into a crowded street. The first person on whom it falls flips it away onto another who tosses it to a third, and so on until it explodes and burns the last poor fellow before he can get rid of it. Can he sue only the man who passed the squib to him? Only the one who started it all? Anyone along the line whom he can identify —since it may be difficult or impossible to locate the first and last culprits? Can he choose as defendant the one with the most money? With the computer as with the squib, the original or even ultimate source of the damage is not always known. Since a person probably does not know that the computer has his dossier, and almost certainly does not know what is in it nor how many sources of information it has, he may not suspect it was the source of the injury. The whole thing may seem to him no more than bad luck.

Considerable research would be required to locate the origin of deposits in many data banks. The Federal government alone has 3,000 computers and sells the information in many of them to anyone who asks for it, as do states and private companies. The data can range from the trivial to the tremendous, from utterly false but completely damning rumors to a meticulously accurate history of a lifetime's experiences, utterances, and contacts. The computer does not discriminate be-

tween fact and fancy. It "remembers" everything and on demand reports everything. Linked to other computers, it can be
programmed to store data on everybody in the country. Already some cover forty or fifty million citizens while presumably the Census Bureau takes in all 200,000,000.

Neither government nor business could operate on anything approaching their present scale without the computer or
some equally efficient reservoir of information. So any notion of
outlawing the machine is impractical. This is nothing new. The
country has learned from the whole history of modern technology that inventions—steam engines, internal combustion engines, electricity, the telegraph, the telephone, wireless communications, airplanes—each required Law to devise regulations to control abuses and to maximize beneficial uses. Today
Law herself employs the computer. In 1968, the U.S. Court of
Appeals for the Tenth Circuit, which sits in Denver, ran a test
of computerizing its calendar and system for retrieving cases.
The court used a computer in Santa Monica, California, and
terminal equipment in Falls Church, Virginia, an extreme but
not unusual geographical spread. The conclusion drawn was
that a trial court would benefit even more than an appellate
tribunal. Against these benefits, Law now begins to weigh the
risks.

The computer's threat to men's right to be let alone is
reminiscent of the situation that prevailed nearly ninety years
ago when two imaginative and indignant young lawyers virtually invented the law of privacy. At the same time, they
bequeathed to us a few ideas of what to do about today's
potential menace. The two were Louis D. Brandeis, the future
Supreme Court Justice, and Samuel D. Warren, who had been
graduated first and second from the Harvard Law School in
1877. They formed a partnership in Boston in 1879. When
Warren married in 1883, the tribulations that led them to state
the law of privacy began. Both Warren and his bride, Mabel
Bayard, were members of Boston's aristocracy. With the spread

of literacy and improvements in the printing press, a large market had grown up for gossip about the private doings of the rich. One of the papers that specialized in what it called "blue blood items" was *The Saturday Evening Gazette*, and it chronicled in a most offensive manner the parties that the Warrens gave and attended.

"The press is overstepping in every direction the obvious bounds of propriety and decency," the partners wrote. "Gossip is no longer the resource of the idle and the vicious, but has become a trade, which is pursued with industry as well as effrontery. To satisfy a prurient taste, the details of sexual relations are spread broadcast in the columns of the daily papers. To occupy the indolent, column upon column is filled with idle gossip, which can only be procured by intrusion upon the domestic circle."

Legal redress was then confined to injuries from defamation but not injured feelings resulting from the press's impertinence. Such a vacuum was abhorrent to young men with lofty professional ideals. This pair went to their books and deduced that in the common law men had a right to "an inviolate personality." They quoted a standard work by an eminent authority, Judge Thomas M. Cooley: "The right to one's person may be said to be a right to be let alone." Brandeis and Warren put the results of their study and their talk into an article, "The Right to Privacy," published in *The Harvard Law Review* on December 15, 1890. Their conclusion was this:

"The common law has always recognized a man's house as his castle, impregnable, often, even to its own officers engaged in the execution of its commands. Shall the courts thus close the front entrance to constituted authority, and open wide the back door to idle and prurient curiosity?"

This may sound very persuasive today, but not all judges accepted it at the time. Within a year, the article was mentioned in a New York lawsuit that restrained a drug manufacturer from using a doctor's name without his consent. Another

New York judge decided in favor of an actor who in 1893 objected to having his picture published in a newspaper. But higher courts did not immediately speak, and the right to privacy won its way into established Law only after some vicissitudes, of which one of the most famous was *Roberson v. Rochester Folding Box Company.*

Abigail Roberson was a pretty upstate New Yorker who in 1902 was so horrified when she saw her photograph in an advertisement of a "Flour of the Family" that she suffered nervous shock, physical illness, and a sense of humiliation. She sued the box company, which had used her portrait without permission, for $15,000. She won in the lower courts, but the state's highest tribunal reversed the judgment by a vote of four to three. The minority referred twice to the Brandeis-Warren article, once saying it had presented the novel idea of privacy "with attractiveness and no inconsiderable ability," and then calling it a clever analysis of English cases. But four judges disagreed categorically with what the article said these cases proved. Poor Abigail lost her award, but her cause and her face had aroused so much public sympathy that the New York Legislature adopted the Brandeis-Warren theory in a statute on privacy. Other state courts preferred the New York minority view that Brandeis and Warren were right, and in still other states the legislatures acted, so that by the time computers arrived to upset the applecart, the law of privacy was pretty firmly established.

Whether brought about by judicial interpretation of the common law or by statute, protection of the right to be let alone was Law's response to popular demand. The machine's new challenge to privacy will be met in the same way. If New Yorkers retain the sentiment their grandfathers displayed when Abigail was so sadly wronged by the Rochester Folding Box Company, courts and legislatures will curb the computer. If people cease to believe their privacy is worth protecting, they will lose it. But on the assumption that enough will still prefer to keep some areas of their lives free from the intrusion of snoops—whether the snoops are inspired by bureaucratic zeal or private profit—Law has some reserves of power that may yet be used.

Court decisions on the issues so far have concerned the individual's right to prevent disclosure of his dossier or parts of it. Judges have been fairly narrow in their definition of privacy and who is entitled to it, so that to enjoy it legally a man must be very private indeed. Brandeis and Warren themselves had excluded the activities of a public figure in all areas that impinged upon his public life. But who is a public figure? Even fleeting exposure to fame is enough to warrant intrusion. Becoming what editors consider newsworthy may be enough to strip a man of his right to be let alone, and leave him fair game the rest of his life. Consider what might be called The Case of the Prodigy's Publicity.

When William James Sidis was a little boy, he was a mathematics marvel of such attainments that at the age of 11 he lectured on four-dimensional bodies to learned professors, and at 16 was graduated from Harvard. His father had pushed him so relentlessly into notoriety that he developed a passion for being let alone, gave up study, got an obscure job as a clerk, lived in a drab Boston hall bedroom, and saw as few people as possible. His chief hobby was collecting streetcar transfers. He had removed himself as completely from public view as a man can, but in 1937, a quarter of a century after his last notice by the press, *The New Yorker* magazine published a biographical sketch of him. It was a sad story, from the ruthless exploitation of his talent when he was a child to the dinginess of his mature struggle to lose himself in the anonymity of a low-paid routine job. Thus flung back into the limelight, although briefly, Sidis sued, and a three-man Federal court in New York heard his plea.

In their decision, the judges paid their respects to the inventors of this branch of law— "All comment upon the right of privacy must stem from the famous article by Warren and Brandeis." They agreed that under the standards there set forth Sidis's right of privacy had been invaded. But, they added, "at some point the public interest in obtaining information becomes dominant over the individual's desire for privacy." They admitted they were not prepared to define precisely when that happened.

"At least," they ruled, "we would permit limited scrutiny of the 'private' life of any person who has achieved, or *has had thrust upon him,* the questionable and indefinable status of a 'public figure.'"

That status persists through the years for men like Sidis because of the "popular news interest" in the fate of an unusual personality. The court carefully refrained from expressing an opinion as to whether "newsworthiness" would always be a defense. But it is in the case of a child prodigy. Sidis's "interest in mental and emotional tranquility . . . however real, is one not yet protected by law."

Of course, the computer's invasion of privacy goes beyond impairment of mental and emotional tranquility, and most of its victims are by no stretch of the imagination public figures. But those other interests are not protected by law either, and the widening pervasiveness of the machine's records has brought forth some cries of alarm that perhaps presage Law's intervention.

As of this writing, one possible source of Federal regulation is the Senate Subcommittee on Human Rights, whose chairman is Sam J. Ervin of North Carolina, a former judge, one of the earliest critics of the proliferation of unrestrained, mushrooming data banks. He has disclosed the fact that hardly an agency in Washington does not want to have on file everything anyone knows about the people who might affect its work or have some dealings with it—and even on some who have nothing to do with it. The Internal Revenue Service builds up a data bank on taxpayers, the State Department on passport applicants, the FBI on criminals (and two or three times as many other people), the Secret Service on persons who might harass or embarrass officials the Service protects, the Housing and Urban Development Department on loan applicants, the Department of Agriculture on farmers, the Armed Forces on those who have served in them or done business with them, the Census Bureau on everybody—to mention just a few whose data-collection activities have recently been questioned.

The menace in all this—and the merit, too, it must be remembered—is the ease with which the computer can exchange information so that the dossier of any individual can be drawn from all of them at once. Does a constable in Kansas want to know if a suspect he picked up has been convicted before or is wanted elsewhere? The FBI computer gives him the man's complete criminal record. No technological or legal reason exists why the computer should not give also his credit rating, marital status, school records, intelligence and aptitude test scores, job history, drinking and smoking habits, opinions on anything from sex to politics, religion, medical history, sporting proclivities, past and present associates, and taste in clothes, reading, drama, and television. Suppose the constable wants the same information about a visiting lecturer at the high school or an applicant for the post of librarian or just someone about whom he is curious? Law does not forbid his asking nor the FBI from complying. Each agency sets up its own rules about this, and some of them are pretty strict.

Hardly anyone wants government to refrain from gathering personal data, whether about spies and crime or taste in food and clothes. Nor is it easy to say where some agencies should stop. The Secret Service has been bitterly criticized for gathering dossiers on people it only suspects of wanting to "embarrass" a government official. Yet many commentators took both the Service and the FBI severely to task for not having kept better track of Lee Harvey Oswald. As a practical matter, it is hard to see how either of these agencies could do the job expected of them if they were forbidden to keep files on anyone they considered dangerous. They would be remiss if they did not err on the side of completeness. Would you want to be responsible for deciding that any given individual is incapable of assassinating a President?

The real concern of Law, and the rest of us, is the accuracy of what is fed to the computer and the use made of it. Files are often replete with wild, malicious rumors that have no relation to reality. Yet the correction or elimination of error is admittedly a rarity. Whether the courts can enforce a remedy in the absence of legislation is questionable.

One judge in the District of Columbia has ruled that the FBI need not expunge from its criminal record file the fact that a man was arrested in California in 1965 on suspicion of burglary. The police there found no evidence on which to hold him, and he was released. But anyone who asks for his record will get the 1965 report. This is no isolated case. FBI reports show that of all adults arrested for the crimes of grand larceny, robbery and burglary, from a fifth to a third are acquitted or the charges are dropped without a trial. Yet one hardly wants to deprive the police of access to arrest records. The harm is in irresponsible use of the material and its release to data banks that could misuse it.

Whether one objects more to being data-banked by a government agency or private enterprise is a matter of taste. The computers in private hands are quite as little regulated. Their owners are equally prone to error and equally reluctant to make corrections. Damages resulting from erroneous credit information may be easier to collect in court than those stemming from faulty government records, as the verdict against the credit-rating company in 1969 indicates. Yet few of those who study the subject think that in the private sector the public is adequately protected, although many companies have procedures to safeguard privacy.

Such a feeling inspired the Federal Communications Commission to launch a special Computer Inquiry in 1966 when it asserted: "This personal and proprietary information must remain free from unauthorized invasion or disclosure." But in 1969, the Commission said it needed more information before it could even decide whether to attempt regulation, let alone suggest what the regulations might be.

A common complaint is that men have been denied credit because someone fed the wrong name or fact or rumor into the computer. As more and more everyday transactions are completed without cash, the demand for review and correction of the data bank's contents rises. Anyone who has been through the frustrating experience of trying to catch up with a department store error—say a little matter of a decimal that says you owe $1,000 instead of $10.00—can testify to the need. The computer cannot read letters of complaint, and simply goes on sending out the bill on whatever increasingly belligerent or threatening scale its programmer sets. No one who can be reached by telephone has anything to do with the monster or any control over it. Meantime, the thing may be informing all the other computers in its network that so-and-so is a deadbeat. The nearest thing to a remedy in Law, adopted in a few states including Illinois, is that a victim who learns about an error in his file maintained by a credit company or employe investigative outfit can compel the company to delete it. Since no company is obliged to reveal what is in its files and almost never does so voluntarily, this provision profits very few individuals on whom dossiers are kept. So far as we can find, no legal restrictions on who may buy the dossier exist, whether companies looking into credit or private persons looking for scandal. In England, Law requires the companies to send their reports to the subject without being asked.

Anyone can set up as a specialist in this business and begin selling computerized data-bank information derived from whatever sources seem interesting, saleable, and easy to tap. A particularly lucrative branch is the one on which prospective employers can draw for information about present or prospective workers. One such bank is said to have six million names stored in its computer, complete with what its advertising calls the "largest private collection on revolutionary activities in America." Another company concentrates on dossiers of individuals—it claims seven million—who in its judgment are anti-American or anti-Christian, or have spoken or written something that indicates such sentiments. Both of these are chiefly useful as blacklists, and they make those of the Joe McCarthy era look picayune.

The computer can set up embarrassing situations that involve no villainy by anyone. A man borrows a check from a friend because he left his own at home or in the office. He scratches out the name of the friend's bank, writes in the name of his own, and makes it out to a merchant for a purchase of several hundred dollars. A couple of weeks later, the friend receives a notice from his own bank that he is overdrawn, or a check that a colleague cashed for him bounces. The borrower, the friend and the merchant have forgotten, if they ever knew, that these checks are handled by a computer. The machine does not read the name of the bank, only those oddly shaped code numbers at the bottom of the check, which are printed in magnetic ink.

A law suit suggestive of how our own courts might place responsibility for such a mishap was settled in England in 1965. A bookmaker made out a check on the Westminster Bank for £2,500 drawn to cash. He used a blank issued by one branch, but crossed out the branch name and wrote in that of another. He had accounts in both. Then, for what reason does not appear in the record, he ordered the second branch to stop payment, carefully describing the check and the fact that he had written the branch name in place of the printed one. Of course, the computer read the magnetic-ink code numbers and sent the check to the branch they dictated, where it was duly cashed. The bookmaker sued the Westminster Bank to recover. The bank's defense was that the depositor's checkbook carried a notice in small type restricting the use of the checks to the particular account identified by the code number. Such fine print, said the court, was not sufficiently valid to bind the customer, and the bank should pay the bookmaker.

In this country, the computer has inspired tentative legislation on both Federal and state levels, although the machine is not mentioned. These statutes require an employer to tell a job applicant whom he rejects the source and nature of any adverse report on his credit or past record or opinions that caused the rejection. The main effect seems to be that employers manage to base their rejection on something other than the reports from data banks. Companies that supply information or conduct investigations of prospective employes for large corporations opposed even this move toward regulation of their business.

Professor Arthur Miller of the University of Michigan Law School is a leading authority in this field. He has argued that the First Amendment may not apply. Data banks seldom broadcast their contents to anyone except customers. Professor Miller thinks that anyway they "may be more suited to institutional control of the people than vice versa." This aspect, as it becomes more widely known, leads him to believe that control of the swollen data banks may become attractive politically, an issue that would be good for votes.

Edward J. Grenier, Jr., a Washington, D. C., lawyer, has proposed that the data bank industry itself protect the public's privacy under an act of Congress. Grenier wants the industry, with congressional authorization, to organize its own agency to do these things: (1) Establish and supervise standards for all computerized data-bank operations, apparently along the lines of the New York Stock Exchange in the securities business. (2) License computer systems that handle data about individuals or data that belongs to other companies. (3) Draw up a code of conduct for programmers and other key computer personnel, giving the agency power of discipline, even to the point of expulsion from the industry after flagrant violations.

The proposed act of Congress would assign a government agency, perhaps the FCC, or create a new one to review the industry's standards before they go into effect. While the author does not say so, one of the achievements of his self-regulatory agency might be to forestall more drastic government controls over the correction and dissemination if not the collection of computerized data. Professor Miller prefers public regulation of a public utility, which in some respects the data banks have become, so that "recorded personal information conform to minimal standards of accuracy." He has not been optimistic, for in his book, *Computers, Data Banks, and Dossiers,* he expresses doubt that Congress has sufficient knowledge to deal with an Executive Branch that already operates something like three thousand computers.

Of course, this industry, like every other that sprang from technological progress, cries out that regulation will destroy it and all the immense benefits it brings to the people. This plea for *laissez faire* was long ago proved wrong in every other branch of business. Regulations are more likely to strengthen than to weaken the dealers in personal information. Professor Alan Westin of Columbia University, who is making a special study of the political implications of data banks, points out that computers can be programmed to protect privacy as well as destroy it, to promote truth rather than perpetuate falsehoods. One way would be to have the computer automatically notify the subject that his file has been sent to such-and-such persons or firms or government agencies and tell him why they wanted the information. It could be programmed to send to the central agency that Grenier has proposed the name of each seeker of information and the purpose to which he proposed to put it. The machine could be ordered to give its records to one class of inquirers and withhold them from another. All that is likely to happen only if Law requires it.

The misuse of industrial and commercial information concerns some lawyers and businessmen at least as much as the invasion of individual privacy. The states no doubt will experiment with legislation to minimize this, whether the industry sets up an agency or not. More than one control mechanism would be needed for various computer systems. The machine that a huge corporation sets up to program its manufacturing processes, order shipments in and out of warehouses, pay employes, and bill customers presents a different legal situation than one that collects and distributes credit information about customers to retailers. For all systems that have anything to do with the public, the English law may serve as a model, or at least a starting point. Data banks in Great Britain must register with a central agency, send each person on whom they have records a copy of that information and the names of companies or individuals to whom it is supplied, and correct or expunge errors.

Similar legislation in this country probably would not bind government agencies strictly on the collection of misinformation. One would expect any limitations on them to be directed to the use they make of both facts and rumors. Law generally takes the position that it will tolerate the embarrassment or inconvenience of individual citizens if the welfare of all citizens benefits, but not the invasion of constitutional rights.

This is a never-ending conflict. The boundaries of that tolerance shift constantly with the changing fears, hopes, and prejudices of the people. During and just before World War II, the public properly tolerated extensive surveillance to keep tabs on enemy spies and sympathizers, such as active or passive pro-Nazis, before we entered the war. At the end of that conflict, the public also quite properly tolerated the suppression of lists of people found during that surveillance to have offered help to Germany, so long as they did nothing to harm this country after hostilities began.

As society becomes increasingly computerized, Law concerns itself with more than privacy, even more than protecting business secrets. Automation in communications, the press, and entertainment will soon put the whole output of all these at a man's fingertips as he sits in his home. Sufficiently sophisticated computers will make it possible for him to talk back to "Big Brother" wherever that potentate may be—in business, in the mass media, in government. The householder will dial the news, sports, shows, music, lectures, discussions, or pictures that he wants. Law will have something to say about who has access to him and to whom he has access. The competition for his attention will produce nice legal questions, some of which have already been foreshadowed in the development of broadcasting. The licensing of channels to men's minds and who shall pay for the operation will be fought out in legislatures and courts as well as in the marketplace.

We are also heading toward an economic system in which cash and checks will be obsolete. A glorified credit card or Social Security number could be used for all transactions from buying a house to paying for a meal to collecting salaries or dividends. Computers would not only send the bills to the bank but pay them and keep the individual informed as to the state of his account. Law will be drawn into this highly automated system not only to regulate the programmers and operators but to establish liability for the inevitable mistakes. A suggestion of how Law might meet this last challenge is contained in what is often cited as a leading bank case, *Peterson v. First National Bank*, decided in Idaho in 1961.

Banks are governed in part by the Uniform Commercial Code, which says among other things that "no agreement may disclaim a bank's responsibility for its own lack of good faith or failure to exercise ordinary care or can limit the measure of damages for such lack or failure." The First National Bank gave Peterson's employer information about his financial condition without getting his permission to do so. He sued, claiming the bank had invaded his privacy. The court said not so; privacy was not an issue, but the bank had violated an implied contract that it would not divulge anything about a depositor's account without his consent.

When everything about every monetary transaction is computerized, and one computer can be hooked up to all the others whose owners might be interested, Law may expand the responsibility for maintaining good faith and exercising ordinary care from commercial banks to data banks. In this branch of technology, as in many others, Law may seem to be the plodding tortoise, looking back to precedents and past authorities, while Science leaps ahead to ever new techniques and processes. In the fairy tale, no one has any doubts as to which legendary animal will win the unequal race; the poor hare hasn't a chance. In real life, the outcome must always remain uncertain. For the legal regulation of the computer and technology in general is not decided by either Law or Science, or even by both together. In this country, the people still reign, whether by the rules they demand or by abdicating their power. So a book such as this, written for people, fittingly ends with a question rather than an answer:

How far do *you* want Law to go in setting guidelines for Science and the application of scientific discoveries?

As you ponder your answer, remember that these chapters have presented samples of confrontations between Science and Law, not a complete catalog. Most lawyers and many laymen will think of cases and situations we have omitted. We venture that more examples would only underscore the toughness of our question.

| Table of Cases

237

| Sources

The principal published sources for this book, other than reports of cases and newspaper or magazine articles cited in the text, were:

Arizona Law Review, Summer, 1968, "Air Pollution."

Brooks, Eugene, "Legal Aspects of the Lunar Landings," *International Lawyer*, April, 1970.

Bulletin of the Atomic Scientists, April, 1970, "The Chemistry and Cost of Contamination."

Bulletin of the Atomic Scientists, September, 1970, Miscellany of correspondence on radiation and atomic energy.

Cardozo, Benjamin N., *The Growth of the Law*, Yale Univ. Press, 1924.

Carter, Luther J., "Environmental Pollution," *Science*, Dec. 22, 1969.

Clarke, John J., "Automation," *Banking Law Journal*, Spring, 1970.

Corday, Eliot, "Life-Death in Human Transplants," *American Bar Association Journal*, July, 1969.

D'Amato, Anthony A., "Environmental Degradation and Legal Action," *Bulletin of the Atomic Scientists*, March, 1970.

Delagu, Orlando E., "Legal Aspects of Air Pollution Control," *Wisconsin Law Review*, 1969.

Environmental Law Review, July, 1970.

Ernst, Morris L. and David Loth, *How High Is Up*, Bobbs-Merrill, Indianapolis, 1964.

Georgetown Law Review, November, 1969, "Computers and Administrative Investigations."

Gindler, Burton J., *Water Pollution and Quality Control*, Allen Smith Co. 1967.

Glass, Bentley, "Presidential Address to the American Association for the Advancement of Science," December, 1970.

Green, Harold F., "The New Technology: A View from the Law," *Bulletin of the Atomic Scientists*, November, 1969.

Grenier, Edward J. Jr., "Computers and Privacy," *Duke Law Journal*, June, 1970.

Halacy, D. S. Jr., *The Weather Changers*, Harper & Row, 1968.

Hardin, Garrett, "To Twinkle a Star: The Cost of Intervention in Nature," *Bulletin of the Atomic Scientists*, January, 1970.

International Lawyer, October, 1968, "Ad Hoc Committee on Seabed and Ocean Floor."

Law and Contemporary Problems, 1969, "Symposium on Communications."

Leef, Alexander, M.D., "Social Consequences of New Developments in Medicine," *Bulletin of the Atomic Scientists*, January, 1970.

Loth, Alan, "Nuisance Law and Pollution," Unpublished manuscript, 1970.

Martin, Robert and Lloyd Symington, "A Guide to the Air Quality Act of 1967," *Law and Contemporary Problems*, Spring, 1968.

Meeker, Leonard C., "The First Decade of Law in Space," *International Lawyer*, January, 1969.

Miller, Arthur R., "Personal Privacy in the Computer Age," *Michigan Law Review*, April, 1969.

Miller, Arthur Selwyn, "Science vs. Law," *Buffalo Law Review*, Spring, 1968.

Nehman, Jerzy, "Areal Spread of the Effect of Cloud Seeding at the Whitetop Experiment," *Science*, March 28, 1969.

Novick, S. N., *The Careless Atom*, Houghton Mifflin, Boston, 1969.

Pollack, Lawrence W., "Legal Boundaries of Air Pollution Control," *Law and Contemporary Problems*, Spring, 1968.

Robinson, George S., "Earth Exposure to Extraterrestrial Matter," *International Lawyer*, April, 1971.

Rosenfeld, Albert, *The Second Genesis—The Coming Control of Life*, Prentice-Hall, N.Y., 1969.

Shapiro, Barbara J., "Law and Science in Seventeenth Century England," *Stanford Law Review*, April, 1969.

Stoever, William A., "The Race for the Seabed," *International Lawyer*, April, 1970.

Taubenfeld, Howard J., *Controlling the Weather*, Dunellen Pub. Co., 1970.

Taubenfeld, Rita F. and Howard J., "The International Implications of Weather Modification," *Bulletin of the Atomic Scientists*, January, 1969.

Toffler, Alvin, *Future Shock*, Random House, N.Y., 1970.

Van Pankuys, Haro F., "Aircraft Hijacking and International Law," *Columbia Journal of Transnational Law*, Spring, 1970.

Whittaker, William L. and John T. McDermott, "Computer Technology in an Appellate Court," *Judicature*, June, 1970.

| Index